Zanzibar Tales

Zanzibar Tales

Told by natives of the coast of East Africa

Translated from the original Swahili by
George Bateman

Illustrated by Walter Bobbett

Gallery Publications
Zanzibar

Published in 2006 by
Gallery Publications
P.O. Box 3181, Zanzibar
e-mail: gallery@swahilicoast.com

ISBN 9987 667 57 0

First Published in 1901 by A.C. McClurg & Co

Edited by Mark Wilson

CONTENTS

TO MY READERS

Thirty years ago Central Africa was what people who are fond of airing their learning would call a terra incognita. To-day its general characteristics are pretty well known. Then, as now, the little island of Zanzibar, situated just south of the equator, on the east coast, was the starting place of all expeditions into the interior, and Unguja (pronounced Oo-ngoo'jah), the big town of that island, the place where the preparations for plunging into the unknown were made.

At that period these expeditions consisted, almost without exception, of caravans loaded with beads and cotton cloth, which were exchanged among the inland tribes for elephants' tusks and slaves, for Unguja boasted the only, and the last, open slave-market in the world then.

The few exceptions were a would-be discoverer now and then, or a party of rich white men going to hunt "big game;" that is, travelling hundreds -aye, thousands - of miles, and enduring many hardships, for the momentary pleasure of holding a gun in such a position that when they pulled the trigger the bullet hit such a prominent mark as an elephant or a lion, which was living in its natural surroundings and interfering with no one.

Between you and me, I don't mind remarking that many of their expeditions ended, on their return to Unguja, in the purchase of a few elephants' tusks and wild animal skins in the bazaars of that thriving city, after the method pursued by unsuccessful anglers in civilized countries.

But even the most successful of these hunters, by reason of having followed the few beaten paths known to their guides, never came within miles of such wonderful animals as those described by the tribesmen from the very center of the dark continent. If you have read any accounts of adventure in Africa, you will know that travellers never mention animals of any kind that are gifted with the faculty of speech, or gazelles that are overseers for native princes, or hares that eat flesh. No, indeed; only the native-born know of these; and, judging by the immense and rapid strides civilization is making in those parts, it will not be long before such wonderful specimens of zoology will be as extinct as the ichthyosaurus, dinornis, and other poor creatures who never dreamed of the awful names that would be applied to them when they were too long dead to show their resentment.

As to the truth of these tales, I can only say that they were told to me, in Zanzibar, by negroes whose ancestors told them to them, who had received them from their ancestors, and so back; so that the praise for their accuracy, or the blame for their falsity, lies with the first ancestor who set them going.

You may think uncivilized negroes are pretty ignorant people, but the white man who is supposed to have first told the story of "The House that Jack Built" was a mighty poor genius compared with the unknown originator of "Goso, the Teacher," who found even inanimate things that were endowed with speech, which the pupils readily understood and were not astonished to hear; while "Puss in Boots" was not one-half so clever as the gazelle that ran things for Hamdani. It would be a severe task to rattle off "Goso " as you do "The House that Jack Built."

Don't stumble over the names in these tales; they are very easy. Every one is pronounced exactly as it is spelled, and the accent is always on the last syllable but one; as, Punda, the donkey Hamdani, etc.

Finally, if the perusal of these tales interests you as much as their narration and translation interested me, everything will be satisfactory.

GEORGE W. BATEMAN
CHICAGO
August 1, 1901

I
THE MONKEY, THE SHARK, AND THE WASHERMAN'S DONKEY

Once upon a time Kima, the monkey, and Papa, the shark, became great friends.

The monkey lived in an immense mkuyu tree which grew by the margin of the sea - half of its branches being over the water and half over the land.

Every morning, when the monkey was breakfasting on the kuyu nuts, the shark would put in an appearance under the tree and call out, "Throw me some food, my friend," with which request the monkey complied most willingly.

This continued for many months, until one day Papa said, "Kima, you have done me many kindnesses: I would like you to go with me to my home, that I may repay you."

"How can I go? " said the monkey; "we land

beasts can not go about in the water."

"Don't trouble yourself about that," replied the shark; "I will carry you. Not a drop of water shall get to you."

"Oh, all right, then," said Mr. Kima; "let's go."

When they had gone about half-way the shark stopped, and said: "You are my friend. I will tell you the truth."

"Why, what is there to tell?" asked the monkey, with surprise.

"Well, you see, the fact is that our sultan is very sick, and we have been told that the only medicine that will do him any good is a monkey's heart."

"Well," exclaimed Kima, "you were very foolish not to tell me that before we started!"

"How so?" asked Papa.

But the monkey was busy thinking up some means of saving himself, and made no reply.

"Well?" said the shark, anxiously; "why don't you speak?"

"Oh, I've nothing to say now. It's too late. But if you had told me this before we started, I might have brought my heart with me."

"What? Haven't you your heart here?"

"Huh!" ejaculated Kima; "don't you know about us? When we go out we leave our hearts in the trees, and go about with only our bodies. But I see you don't believe me. You think I'm scared. Come on; let's go to your home, where you can kill me and search for my heart in vain."

The shark did believe him, though, and exclaimed, "Oh, no; let's go back and get your heart."

"Indeed, no," protested Kima; "let us go on to your home."

But the shark insisted that they should go back, get the heart, and start afresh.

At last, with great apparent reluctance, the monkey consented, grumbling sulkily at the unnecessary trouble he was being put to.

When they got back to the tree, he climbed up in a great hurry, calling out, "wait there, Papa, my friend, while I get my heart, and we'll start off properly next time."

When he had got well up among the branches, he sat down and kept quite still.

After waiting what he considered a reasonable length of time, the shark called, “Come along, Kima!” But Kima just kept still and said nothing.

In a little while he called again: “Oh, Kima! let’s be going.”

At this the monkey poked his head out from among the upper branches and asked, in great surprise, “Going where?”

“To my home, of course.”

“Are you mad?” queried Kima.

“Mad? Why, what do you mean?” cried Papa.

“What’s the matter with you?” said the monkey. “Do you take me for a washerman’s donkey?”

“What peculiarity is there about a washerman’s donkey?”

“It is a creature that has neither heart nor ears.”

The shark, his curiosity overcoming his haste, thereupon begged to be told the story of the washerman’s donkey, which the monkey related as follows:

"Miss Punda, I am sent to ask your hand in marriage"

"A washerman owned a donkey, of which he was very fond. One day, however it ran away, and took up its abode in the forest, where it led a lazy life, and consequently grew very fat.

"At length Sungura, the hare, by chance passed that way, and saw Punda, the donkey.

"Now, the hare is the most cunning of all beasts -if you look at his mouth you will see that he is always talking to himself about everything.

"So when Sungura saw Punda he said to himself. 'My, this donkey is fat!' Then he went and told Simba, the lion.

"As Simba was just recovering from a severe illness, he was still so weak that he could not go hunting. He was consequently pretty hungry.

"Said Mr. Sungura I'll bring enough meat tomorrow for both of us to have a great feast, but you will have to do the killing.'

"All right, good friend,' exclaimed Simba joyfully; 'you're very kind.'

"So the hare scampered off to the forest, found the donkey, and said to her, in his most courtly manner, 'Miss Punda, I am sent to ask your hand in marriage.'

"By whom?' simpered the donkey.

"By Simba, the lion.'

"The donkey was greatly elated at this, and exclaimed: 'Let's go at once. This is a first-class offer."

"They soon arrived at the lion's home, were cordially invited in, and sat down. Sungura gave Simba a signal with his eyebrow, to the effect that this was the promised feast, and that he would wait outside. Then he said to Punda: 'I must leave you for a while to attend to some private business. You stay here and converse with your husband that is to be.'

"As soon as Sungura got outside, the lion sprang at Punda, and they had a great fight. Simba was kicked very hard, and he struck with his claws as well as his weak health would permit him. At last the donkey threw the lion down, and ran away to her home in the forest.

"Shortly after, the hare came back, and called, 'Haya! Simba, have you got it?'

"I have not got it,' growled the lion; she kicked me and ran away; but I warrant you I made her feel pretty sore, though I'm not - strong.'

"Oh, well,' remarked Sungura; 'don't put yourself out of the way about it.'

"Then Sungura waited many days, until the lion and the donkey were both well and strong when he said: 'What do you think now, Simba? Shall I bring you your meat?'

"'Ay,' growled the lion, fiercely; 'bring it to me. I'll tear it in two pieces !'

"So the hare went off to the forest, where the donkey welcomed him and asked the news.

"'You are invited to call again and see your lover,' said Sungura.

"'Oh, dear!' cried Punda; 'that day you took me to him he scratched me awfully. I'm afraid to go near him now.'

"'Ah, pshaw!' said Sungura; 'that's nothing. That's only Simba's way of caressing.'

"'Oh, well,' said the donkey, 'let's go.'

"So off they started again; but as soon as the lion caught sight of Punda he sprang upon her and tore her in two pieces.

" When the hare came up, Simba said to

him: 'Take this meat and roast it. As for myself, all I want is the heart and ears.'

"'Thanks,' said Sungura. Then he went away and roasted the meat in a place where the lion could not see him, and he took the heart and ears and hid them. Then he ate all the meat he needed, and put the rest away.

" Presently the lion came to him and said, 'Bring me the heart and ears.'

"'Where are they?' said the hare.

"'What does this mean?' growled Simba.

"'Why, didn't you know this was a washerman's donkey?'

"'Well, what's that to do with there being no heart or ears?

"'For goodness' sake, Simba, aren't you old enough to know that if this beast had possessed a heart and ears it wouldn't have come back the second time?'

"Of course the lion had to admit that what Sungura, the hare, said was true.

"And now," said Kima to the shark, "you want to make a washerman's donkey of me. Get out of there, and go home by yourself. You are

not going to get me again, and our friendship is ended.
Good-bye, Papa."

II
THE HARE AND THE LION

One day Sungura, the hare, roaming through the forest in search of food, glanced up through the boughs of a very large calabash tree, and saw that a great hole in the upper part of the trunk was inhabited by bees; thereupon he returned to town in search of some one to go with him and help to get the honey.

As he was passing the house of Buku, the big rat, that worthy gentleman invited him in. So he went in, sat down, and remarked, "My father has died, and has left me a hive of honey. I would like you to come and help me to eat it."

Of course Buku jumped at the offer, and he and the hare started off immediately.

When they arrived at the great calabash tree, Sungura pointed out the bees' nest and said, "Go on; climb up." So, taking some straw with them, they climbed up to the nest, lit the

Buku and the hare started off immediately

straw, smoked out the bees, put out the fire, and set to work eating the honey.

In the midst of the feast, who should appear at the foot of the tree but Simba the lion? Looking up, and seeing them eating, he asked, "Who are you?"

Then Sungura whispered to Buku, "Hold your tongue; that old fellow is crazy." But in a very little while Simba roared out angrily: "Who are you, I say? Speak, I tell you!" This made Buku so scared that he blurted out, "It's only us!"

Upon this the hare said to him: "You just wrap me up in this straw, call to the lion to keep out of the way, and then throw me down. Then you'll see what will happen."

So Buku, the big rat, wrapped Sungura, the hare, in the straw, and then called to Simba, the lion, "stand back; I'm going to throw this straw down and then I'll come down myself." When Simba stepped back out of the way, Buku threw down the straw, and as it lay on the ground Sungura crept out and ran away while the lion was looking up.

After waiting a minute or two, Simba roared out, “Well, come down, I say! and, there being no help for it, the big rat came down.

As soon as he was within reach, the lion caught hold of him, and asked, “Who was up there with you?”

“Why,” said Buku, “Sungura, the hare. Didn’t you see him when I threw him down?”

“Of course I didn’t see him,” replied the lion, in an incredulous tone, and, without wasting further time, he ate the big rat, and then searched around for the hare, but could not find him.

Three days later, Sungura called on his acquaintance, Kobe, the tortoise, and said to him, “Let us go and eat some honey”

“Whose honey? inquired Kobe, cautiously.

“My father’s,” Sungura replied.

“Oh, all right; I’m with you,” said the tortoise, eagerly; and away they went.

When they arrived at the great calabash tree they climbed up with their straw, smoked out the bees, sat down, and began to eat.

Just then Mr. Simba who owned the honey,

came out again, and, looking up, inquired, "Who are you, up there?"

Sungura whispered to Kobe, "Keep quiet;" but when the lion repeated his question angrily, Kobe became suspicious, and said: "I will speak. You told me this honey was yours; am I right in suspecting that it belongs to Simba?"

So, when the lion asked again, "Who are you?" he answered, "It's only us." The lion said, "Come down, then;" and the tortoise answered, "We're coming."

Now, Simba had been keeping an eye open for Sungura since the day he caught Buku, the big rat, and, suspecting that he was up there with Kobe he said to himself, "I've got him this time, sure."

Seeing that they were caught again, Sungura said to the tortoise: "Wrap me up in the straw, tell Simba to stand out of the way, and then throw me down. I'll wait for you below. He can't hurt you, you know."

"All right," said Kobe; but while he was wrapping the hare up he said to himself: "This fellow wants to run away, and leave me to bear the lion's anger. He shall get caught first." Therefore, when he had bundled him up, he called out, "Sungura is coming!" and threw him down.

So Simba caught the hare, and, holding him with his paw, said, "Now, what shall I do with you?" The hare replied, "It's of no use for you to try to eat me; I'm awfully tough." "What would be the best thing to do with you, then?" asked Simba.

"I think," said Sungura, "you should take me by the tail, whirl me around, and knock me against the ground. Then you may be able to eat me."

So the lion, being deceived, took him by the tail and whirled him around, but just as he was going to knock him on the ground he slipped out of his grasp and ran away, and Simba had the mortification of losing him again.

Angry and disappointed, he turned to the tree and called to Kobe, "You come down, too."

When the tortoise reached the ground, the lion said, "You're pretty hard; what can I do to make you eatable?"

The lion continued rubbing on a piece of rock

"Oh, that's easy," laughed Kobe; "just put me in the mud and rub my back with your paw until my shell comes off."

Immediately on hearing this, Simba carried Kobe to the water, placed him in the mud, and began, as he supposed, to rub his back; but the tortoise had slipped away, and the lion continued rub on a piece of rock until his paws were raw. When he glanced down at them he saw they were bleeding, and, realizing that he had again been outwitted, he said, "Well, the hare has done me to-day, but I'll go hunting now until I find him."

So Simba, the lion, set out immediately in search of Sungura, the hare, and as he went along he inquired of every one he met, "Where is the house of Sungura?" But each person he asked answered, "I do not know." For the hare had said to his wife, "Let us move from this house." Therefore the folks in that neighbourhood had no knowledge of his whereabouts. Simba, however, went along, continuing his inquiries, until presently one answered, "That is his house on the top of the mountain."

Without loss of time the lion climbed the mountain, and soon arrived at the place indicated, only to find that there was no one at home. This, however, did not trouble him; on the contrary , saying to himself, "I'll hide myself inside, and when Sungura and his wife come home I'll eat them both," he entered the house and lay down, awaiting their arrival.

Pretty soon along came the hare with his wife, not thinking of any danger; but he very soon discovered the marks of the lion's paws on the steep path. Stopping at once, he said to Mrs. Sungura "You go back, my dear. Simba, the lion, has passed this way, and I think he must be looking for me."

But she replied, "I will not go back; I will follow you, my husband."

Although greatly pleased at this proof of his wife's affection, Sungura said firmly: "No, no; you have friends to go to. Go back."

So he persuaded her, and she went back; but he kept on, following the footmarks, and saw as he had suspected - that they went into his house.

"Ah," said he to himself, "Mr. Lion is inside is he? Then, cautiously going back a little way he called out How d'ye do, house? "How d'ye do?" Waiting moment, he remarked loudly: "Well, this is very strange Every day, as I pass this place, I say, "How d'ye do, house and the house always answers, 'How d'ye do?' There must be some one inside to-day."

When the lion heard this he called out, "How d'ye do?"

Then Sungura burst out laughing, and shouted: "Oho, Mr. Simba *You*'re inside, and I'll bet you want to eat *me*; but first tell me where you ever heard of a house talking!"

Upon this the lion, seeing how he had been fooled, replied angrily, "You wait until I get hold of you; that's all."

"Oh, I think *you*'ll have to do the waiting," cried the hare; and then he ran away, the lion following.

But it was of no use. Sungura completely tired out old Simba, who, saying, "That rascal has beaten me; I don't want to have anything more to do with him," returned to his home under the great calabash tree.

III
THE LION, THE HYENA, AND THE RABBIT

Once upon a time Simba, the lion, Fisi, the hyena, and Kititi the rabbit, made up their minds to go in for a little farming. So they went into the country, made a garden, planted all kinds of seeds, and then came home and rested quite a while.

Then, when the time came when their crops should be about ripe and ready for harvesting, they began to say to each other, "Let's go over to the farm, and see how our crops are coming along."

So one morning early, they started, and, as the garden was a long way off, Kititi, the rabbit, made this proposition:

"While we are going to the farm, let us not stop on the road; and if any one does stop, let him be eaten." His companions not being so cunning as he, and knowing they could outwalk him, readily consented to this arrangement.

Well, off they went; but they had not gone very far when the rabbit stopped.

"Hello!" said Fisi, the hyena, "Kititi has stopped. He must be eaten."

"That's the bargain," agreed Simba, the lion.

"Well," said the rabbit, "I happened to be thinking."

"What about?" cried his partners, with great curiosity.

"I'm thinking," said he, with a grave, philosophical air, "about those two stones, one big, and one little; the little one does not go up, nor does the big one go down."

The lion and the hyena, having stopped to look at the stones, could only say, "Why, really, it's singular; but it's just as you say;" and they all resumed their journey, the rabbit being by this time well rested.

When they had gone some distance the rabbit stopped again.

"Aha!" said Fisi; "Kititi has stopped again.

Said the hyena, "I'm thinking"

Now he *must* be eaten."

"I rather think so," assented Simba.

"Well," said the rabbit, "I was thinking again."

Their curiosity once more aroused, his comrades begged him to tell them his thinking.

"Why," said he, "I was thinking this: When people like us put on new coats, where do the old ones go to?"

Both Simba and Fisi, having stopped a moment to consider the matter, exclaimed together, "Well, I wonder!" and the three went on, the rabbit having again had a good rest.

After a little while the hyena, thinking it about time to show off a little of his philosophy, suddenly stopped.

"Here," growled Simba, "this won't do; I guess we'll have to eat you, Fisi."

"Oh, no," said the hyena I'm thinking."

"What are you thinking about?" they inquired. "Thinking about nothing at all," said he, imagining himself very smart and witty.

"Ah, pshaw!" cried Kititi; "we won't be fooled that way."

So he and Simba ate the hyena.

When they bad finished eating friend, the lion and the rabbit proceeded on their way, and presently came to a place where there was a cave, and here the rabbit stopped.

“H’m!” ejaculated Simba; I’m not so hungry as I was this morning, but I guess I’ll have to find room for you, little Kititi.”

“Oh, I believe not,” replied Kititi; I’m thinking again.”

“Well,” said the lion, “what is it this time?”

Said the rabbit: “I’m thinking about that cave. In olden times our ancestors used to go in here, and go out there, and I think I’ll try and follow in their footsteps.”

So he went in at one end and out at the other end several times.

Then he said to the lion, “fellow, let’s see you try to do that;” and the lion went into the cave but he stuck fast, and could neither go forward nor back out.

In a moment Kititi was on Simba’s back, and began eating him.

After a little time the lion cried, “Oh,

brother, be impartial; come and eat some of the front part of me."

But the rabbit replied, "Indeed, I can't come around in front; I'm ashamed to look you in the face."

So, having eaten all he was able to, he left the lion there, and went and became sole owner of the farm and its crops.

IV
THE KITES AND THE CROWS

One day Kunguru sultan of the crows, sent a letter to Mwewe, sultan of the kites, containing these few words "I want you folks to be my soldiers."

To this brief message Mwewe at once wrote this short reply: "I should say not."

Thereupon, thinking to scare Mwewe, the sultan of the crows sent him word, "If you refuse to obey me I'll make war upon you."

To which the sultan of the kites replied, "That suits me; let us fight, and if you beat us we will obey you, but if we are victors you shall be our servants."

So they gathered their forces and engaged in a great battle and in a little while it became evident that the crows were being badly beaten.

As it appeared certain that, if something were not done pretty quickly, they would all be killed, one old crow, named Jiusi, suddenly proposed that they should fly away.

Directly the suggestion was made it was acted upon, and the crows left their homes and flew far away, where they set up another town. So, when the kites entered the place, they found no one there and they took up their residence in Crowtown.

One day, when the crows had gathered in council, Kunguru stood up and said: "My people, do as I command you, and all will be well. Pluck out some of my feathers and throw me into the town of the kites; then come back and stay here until you hear from me."

Without argument or questioning the crows obeyed their sultan's command.

Kunguru had lain in the street but a short time, when some passing kites saw him and inquired threateningly, "What are you doing here in our town?"

With many a moan he replied, "My companions have beaten me and turned me out of their town because I advised them to obey Mwewe, sultan of the kites."

I
Should
Say
Not

When they heard this they picked him up and took him before the sultan, to whom they said, "We found this fellow lying in the street, and he attributes his involuntary presence in our town to so singular a circumstance that we thought you should hear his story."

Kunguru was then bidden to repeat his statement, which he did, adding the remark that, much as he had suffered, he still held to his opinion that Mwewe was his rightful sultan.

This, of course, made a very favorable impression, and the Sultan said, "You have more sense than all the rest of your tribe put together; I guess you can stay here and live with us."

So Kunguru, expressing much gratitude, settled down, apparently, to spend the remainder of his life with the kites.

One day his neighbours took him to church with them, and when they returned home they asked him, "Who have the best kind of religion, the kites or the crows?"

To which crafty old Kunguru replied, with great enthusiasm, "Oh, the kites, by long odds!"

This answer tickled the kites like anything,

and Kunguru was looked upon as a bird of remarkable discernment.

When almost another week had passed, the sultan of the crows slipped away in the night, went to his own town, and called his people together.

"Tomorrow," said he, "is the great annual religious festival of the kites, and they will all go to church in the morning. Go, now, and get some wood and some fire, and wait near their town until I call you; then come quickly and set fire to the church."

Then he hurried back to Mwewe's town.

The crows were very busy indeed all that night, and by dawn they had an abundance of wood and fire at hand, and were lying in wait near the town of their victorious enemies.

So in the morning every kite went to church. There was not one person left at home except old Kunguru.

When his neighbours called for him they found him lying down. "Why!" they exclaimed with surprise, “are you not going to church to-day?”

“Oh,” said he, I wish I could; but my stomach aches so badly I can’t move! And he groaned dreadfully.

“Ah, poor fellow!” said they; “you will be better in bed;” and they left him to himself.

As soon as everybody was out of sight he flew swiftly to his soldiers and cried, “Come on; they’re all in the church.”

Then they all crept quickly but quietly to the church, and while some piled wood about the door, others applied fire.

The wood caught readily, and the fire was burning fiercely before the kites were aware of their danger; but when the church began to fill with smoke, and tongues of flame shot through the cracks, they tried to escape through the windows. The greater part of them, however, were suffocated, or, having their wings singed, could not fly away, and so were burned to death, among them their sultan, Mwewe; and Kunguru and

They found him lying down

his crows got their old town back again.

From that day to this the kites fly away from the crows.

V
GOSO, THE TEACHER

Once there was a man named Goso, who taught children to read, not in a schoolhouse, but under a calabash tree. One evening, while Goso was sitting under the tree deep in the study of the next day's lessons, Paa, the gazelle, climbed up the tree very quietly to steal some fruit, and in so doing shook off a calabash, which, in falling, struck the teacher on the head and killed him.

When his scholars came in the morning and found their teacher lying dead, they were filled with grief; so, after giving him a decent burial, they agreed among themselves to find the one who had killed Goso, and put him to death.

After talking the matter over they came to the conclusion that the south wind was the offender.

So they caught the south wind and beat it.

But the south wind cried: "Here! I am Kusi, the south wind. Why are you beating me? What have I done?"

And they said: "Yes, we know you are Kusi; it was you who threw down the calabash that struck our teacher Goso. You should not have done it."

But Kusi said, "If I were so powerful would I be stopped by a mud wall ?"

So they went to the mud wall and beat it.

But the mud wall cried: "Here! I am Kiyambaza, the mud wall. Why are you beating me? What have I done?"

And they said: "Yes, we know you are Kiyambaza; it was you who stopped Kusi, the south wind; and Kusi, the south wind, threw down the calabash that struck our teacher Goso. You should not have done it."

But Kiyambaza said, "If I were so powerful would I be bored through by the rat?"

So they went and caught the rat and beat it.

But the rat cried: "Here! I am Panya, the rat. Why are you beating me? What have I done?"

And they said: "Yes, we know you are Panya; it was you who bored through Kiyambaza, the mud wall; which stopped Kusi, the south wind; and Kusi, the south wind, threw down the calabash that struck our teacher Goso. You should not have done it."

But Panya said, "If I were so powerful would I be eaten by a cat?"

So they hunted for the cat, caught it, and beat it.

But the cat cried: "Here! I am Paka, the cat. Why do you beat me? What have I done?"

And they said: "Yes, we know you are Paka; it is you that eats Panya, the rat; who bores through Kiyambaza, the mud wall; which stopped Kusi, the south wind; and Kusi, the south wind, threw down the calabash that struck our teacher Goso. You should not have done it." But Paka said, "If I were so powerful would I be tied by a rope?"

So they took the rope and beat it.

But the rope cried: "Here! I am Kamba, the rope. Why do you beat me? What have I done?"

And they said: "Yes, we know you are Kamba; it is you that ties Paka, the cat; who eats Panya, the rat; who bores through Kiyambaza, the mud wall; which stopped Kusi, the south wind; and Kusi, the south wind, threw down the calabash that struck our teacher Goso. You should not have done it."

But Kamba said, "If I were so powerful would I be cut by a knife?"

So they took the knife and beat it.

But the knife cried: "Her! I am Kisu, the knife. Why do you beat me? What have I done?"

And they said: "Yes, we know you are Kisu; you cut Kamba, the rope; that ties Paka, the cat; who eats Panya, the rat; who bores through Kiyambaza, the mud wall; which stopped Kusi, the south wind; and Kusi, the south wind, threw down the calabash that struck our teacher Goso. You should not have done it."

But Kisu said, "If I were so powerful would I be burned by the fire?"

And they went and beat the fire.

But the fire cried: "Her! I am Moto, the fire. Why do you beat me? What have I done?"

And they said: “Yes, we know you are Moto; you burn Kisu, the knife; that cuts Kamba, the rope; that ties Paka, the cat; who eats Panya, the rat; who bores through Kiyambaza, the mud wall; which stopped Kusi, the south wind; and Kusi, the south wind, threw down the calabash that struck our teacher Goso. You should not have done it.”

But Moto said, “If I were so powerful would I be put out by water?”

And they went to the water and beat it.

But the water cried: “Here! I am Maji, the water. Why do you beat me? What have I done?”

And they said: “Yes, we know you are Maji; you put out Moto, the fire; that burns Kisu, the knife; that cuts Kamba, the rope; that ties Paka, the cat; who eats Panya, the rat; who bores through Kiyambaza, the mud wall; which stopped Kusi, the south wind; and Kusi, the south wind, threw down the calabash that struck our teacher Goso. You should not have done it.”

But Maji said, “If I were so powerful would I be drunk by the ox?”

And they went to the ox and beat it.

But the ox cried: “Here! I am Ng’ombe, the ox. Why do you beat me? What have I done?”

And they said: “Yes, we know you are Ng’ombe; you drink Maji, the water; that puts out Moto, the fire; that burns Kisu, the knife; that cuts Kamba, the rope; that ties Paka, the cat; who eats Panya, the rat; who bores through Kiyambaza, the mud wall; which stopped Kusi, the south wind; and Kusi, the south wind, threw down the calabash that struck our teacher Goso. You should not have done it.”

But Ng’ombe said, “If I were so powerful would I be tormented by the fly?

And they caught a fly and beat it.

But the fly cried: “Here! I am Inzi, the fly. Why do you beat me? What have I done?”

And they said: “Yes, we know you are Inzi; you torment Ng’ombe the ox; who drinks Maji, the water; that puts out Moto, the fire; that burns Kisu, the knife; that cuts Kamba, the rope; that ties Paka, the cat; who eats Panya, the rat; who bores through Kiyambaza, the mud wall; which stopped Kusi, the south wind; and Kusi, the south wind, threw down the calabash that struck our teacher Goso. You should not have done it."

But Inzi said, "If I were so powerful would I be eaten by the gazelle?"

And they searched for the gazelle, and when they found it they beat it.

But the gazelle said: "Here! I am Paa, the gazelle. Why do you beat me? What have I done?"

And they said: "Yes, we know you are Paa; you eat Inzi, the fly; that torments Ng'ombe, the ox; who drinks Maji, the water; that puts out Moto, the fire; that burns Kisu, the knife; that cuts Kamba, the rope; that ties Paka, the cat; who eats Panya, the rat; who bores through Kiyambaza, the mud wall; which stopped Kusi, the south wind; and Kusi, the south wind, threw down the calabash that struck our teacher Goso. You should not have done it."

The gazelle, through surprise at being found out and fear of the consequences of his accidental killing of the teacher, while engaged in stealing, was struck dumb.

Then the scholars said: "Ah! he hasn't a word to say for himself. This is the fellow who threw down the calabash that struck our teacher Goso. We will kill him."

So they killed Paa, the gazelle, and avenged the death of their teacher.

VI
THE APE, THE SNAKE, AND THE LION

Long, long ago there lived, in a village called Kijiji, a woman whose husband died, leaving her with a little baby boy. She worked hard all day to get food for herself and child, but they lived very poorly and were most of the time half-starved.

When the boy, whose name was Mvu Lana?, began to get big, he said to his mother, one day: "Mother, we are always hungry. What work did my father do to support us?

His mother replied: "Your father was a hunter. He set traps, and we ate what he caught in them."

"Oho!" said Mvu Lana; "that's not work; that's fun. I too, will set traps, and see if we can't get enough to eat."

The next day he went into the forest and cut branches from the trees, and returned home in the evening.

The second day he spent making the branches into traps.

The third day he twisted coconut fiber into ropes.

The fourth day he set up as many traps as time would permit.

The fifth day he set up the remainder of the traps.

The sixth day he went to examine the traps, and they had caught so much game, beside what they needed for themselves, that be took a great quantity to the big town of Unguja, where he sold it and bought corn and other things, and the house was full of food; and, as this good fortune continued, be and his mother lived very comfortably.

But after a while, when be went to his traps be found nothing in them day after day.

One morning, however, he found that an ape had been caught in one of the traps, and he was about to kill it, when it said: "Son of Adam, I am Nyani, the ape; do not kill me. Take me out of this trap and let me go. Save me from the rain, that I may come and save you from the sun some day."

So Mvu Lana took him out of the trap and let him go.

When Nyani had climbed up in a tree, he sat on a branch and said to the youth: "For your kindness I will give you a piece of advice: Believe me, men are all bad. Never do a good turn for a man; if you do, he will do you harm at the first opportunity."

The second day, Mvu Lana found a snake in the same trap. He started to the village to give the alarm, but the snake shouted: "Come back, son of Adam; don't call the people from the village to come and kill me. I am Nyoka, the snake. Let me out of this trap, I pray you. Save me from the rain to-day, that I may be able to save you from the sun tomorrow, if you should be in need of help."

So the youth let him go; and as he went he said, "I will return your kindness if I can, but do not trust any man; if you do him a kindness he will do you an injury in return at the first opportunity."

"Mother, we are always hungry"

The third day, Mvu Lana found a lion in the same trap that had caught the ape and the snake, and he was afraid to go near it. But the lion said: “Don’t run. away; I am Simba Kongwe, the very old lion. Let me out of this trap, and I will not hurt you. Save me from the rain, that I may save you from the sun if you should need help.”

So Mvu Lana believed him and let him out of the trap, and Simba Kongwe, before going his way, said: “Son of Adam, you have been kind to me, and I will repay you with kindness if I can; but never do a kindness to a man, or he will pay you back with unkindness.”

The next day a man was caught in the same trap, and when the youth released him, he repeatedly assured him that he would never forget the service he had done him in restoring his liberty and saving his life.

Well, it seemed that he had caught all the game that could be taken in traps, and Mvu Lana and his mother were hungry every day, with nothing to satisfy them, as they had been before. At last he said to his mother, one day:

"Mother, make me seven cakes of the little meal we have left, and I will go hunting with my bow and arrows." So she baked him the cakes, and he took them and his bow and arrows and went into the forest.

The youth walked and walked, but could see no game and finally he found that he had lost his way, and had eaten all his cakes but one.

And he went on and on, not knowing whether he was going away from his home or toward it, until he came to the wildest and most desolate looking wood he had ever seen. He was so wretched and tired that he felt he must lie down and die, when suddenly he heard some one calling him, and looking up he saw Nyani, the ape, who said, "Son of Adam, where are you going?"

"I don't know," replied Mvu Lana, sadly; "I'm lost."

"Well, well," said the ape; "don't worry. Just sit down here and rest yourself until I come back, and I will repay with kindness the kindness you once showed me."

Then Nyani went away off to some gardens

and stole a whole lot of ripe pawpaws and bananas, and brought them to Mvu Lana, and said: "Here's plenty of food for you. Is there anything else you want? Would you like a drink?" And before the youth could answer he ran off with a calabash and brought it back full of water. So the youth ate heartily, and drank all the water he needed, and then each said to the other, "Good-bye, till we meet again," and went their separate ways.

When Mvu Lana had walked a great deal farther without finding which way he should go, he met Simba Kongwe, who asked, "Where are you going, son of Adam?"

And the youth answered, as dolefully as before, "I don't know; I'm lost."

"Come, cheer up," said the very old lion, "and rest yourself here a little. I want to repay with kindness to-day the kindness you showed me on a former day."

So Mvu Lana sat down. Simba Kongwe went away, but soon returned with some game he had caught, and then he brought some fire, and the young man cooked the game and ate it. When

"Where are you going, son of Adam?"

he had finished he felt a great deal better, and they bade each other good-bye for the present, and each went his way.

After he had travelled another very long distance the youth came to a farm, and was met by a very, very old woman, who said to him: "Stranger, my husband has been taken very sick, and I am looking for some one to make him some medicine. Won't you make it?" But he answered: "My good woman, I am not a doctor, I am a hunter, and never used medicine in my life. I cannot help you."

When he came to the road leading to the principal city he saw a well, with a bucket standing near it, and he said to himself: "That's just what I want. I'll take a drink of nice well-water. Let me see if the water can be reached."

As he peeped over the edge of the well, to see if the water was high enough, what should he behold but a great snake, which directly it saw him, said, "Son of Adam, wait a moment." Then it came out of the well and said: "How? Don't you know me?"

"I certainly do not," said the youth, stepping back a little. "Well, well!" said the snake; "I could never forget you. I am Nyoka, whom you released from the trap. You know I said, 'Save me from the rain, and I will save you from the sun.' Now, you are a stranger in the town to which you are going therefore hand me your little bag and I will place in it the things that will be of use to you when you arrive there."

So Mvu Lana gave Nyoka the little bag, and he filled it with chains of gold and silver, and told him to use them freely for his own benefit. Then they parted very cordially.

When the youth reached the city, the first man he met was he whom he had released from the trap, who invited him to go home with him, which he did, and the man's wife made him supper.

As soon as he could get away unobserved, the man went to the sultan and said: "There is a stranger come to my house with a bag full of chains of silver and gold, which he says he got from a snake that lives in a well. But although he pretends to be a man, I know that he is a snake who has power to look like a man.

When the sultan heard this he sent some soldiers who brought Mvu Lana and his little bag before him. When they opened the little bag, the man who was released from the trap persuaded the people that some evil would come out of it, and affect the children of the sultan and the children of the vizier.

Then the people became excited, and tied the hands of Mvu Lana behind him.

But the great snake had come out of the well and arrived at the town just about this time, and he went and lay at the feet of the man who had said all those bad things about Mvu Lana, and when the people saw this they said to that man: "How is this? There is the great snake that lives in the well, and he stays by you. Tell him to go away."

But Nyoka would not stir. So they untied the young man's hands, and tried in every way to make armends for having suspected him of being a wizard.

Then the sultan asked him, "Why should this man invite you to his home and then speak ill of you?"

And Mvu Lana related all that had happened to him and how the ape, the snake, and the lion had cautioned him about the results of doing any kindness for a man.

And the sultan said: "Although men are often ungrateful, they are not always so; only the bad ones. As for this fellow, he deserves to be put in a sack and drowned in the sea. He was treated kindly, and returned evil for good."

Nyoka filled the bag with chains of gold and silver

VII
HAMDANI

Once there was a very poor man, named Hamdani, who begged from door to door for his living sometimes taking things before they were offered him. After a while people became suspicious of him, and stopped giving him anything, in order to keep him away from their houses. So at last he was reduced to the necessity of going every morning to the village dust heap, and picking up and eating the few grains of the tiny little millet seed that he might find there.

One day, as he was scratching and turning over the heap, he found a dime, which he tied up in a corner of his ragged dress, and continued to hunt for millet grains, but could not find one.

"Oh, well," said he, "I've got a dime now; I'm pretty well fixed. I'll go home and take a nap instead of a meal."

So he went to his hut, took a drink of water, put some tobacco in his mouth, and went to sleep.

The next morning, as he scratched in the dust heap, he saw a countryman going along, carrying a basket made of twigs, and he called to him: "Hi, there, countryman what have you in that cage?"

The countryman, whose name was Mohadim, replied, "Gazelles."

And Hamdani called: "Bring them here. Let me see them."

Now there were three well-to-do men standing near; and when they saw the countryman coming to Hamdani they smiled, and said, "You're taking lots of trouble for nothing, Mohadim."

"How's that, gentlemen?" he inquired.

"Why," said they, "that poor fellow has nothing at all. Not a cent."

"Oh, I don't know that," said the countryman; "he may have plenty, for all I know."

"Not he," said they.

"Don't you see for yourself," continued one

of them, “that he is on the dust heap? Every day he scratches there like a hen, trying to get enough grains of millet to keep himself alive. If he had any money, wouldn’t he buy a square meal, for once in his life? Do you think he would want to buy a gazelle? What would he do with it? He can’t find enough food for himself, without looking for any for a gazelle.”

“But,” Mohadim said: “Gentlemen, I have brought some goods here to sell. I answer all who call me, and if any one says ‘Come,’ I go to him. I don’t favour one and slight another; therefore, as this man called me, I’m going to him.”

“All right,” said the first man; “you don’t believe us. Well, we know where he lives, and all about him, and we know that he can’t buy anything.”

“That’s so,” said the second man.

“Perhaps, however, you will see that we were right, after you have a talk with him.”

To which the third man added, “Clouds are a sign of rain, but we have seen no signs of his being about to spend any money.

“All right, gentlemen,” said Mohadim;

"many better-looking people than he call me, and when I show them my gazelles they say, 'Oh, yes, they're very beautiful, but awfully dear; take them away.' So I shall not be disappointed if this man says the same thing. I shall go to him, anyhow."

Then one of the three men said, "Let us go with this man, and see what the beggar will buy."

"Pshaw!" said another; "buy! You talk foolishly. He has not had a good meal in three years, to my knowledge; and a man in his condition doesn't have money to buy gazelles. However, let's go; and if he makes this poor countryman carry his load over there just for the fun of looking at the gazelles, let each of us give him a good hard whack with our walking-sticks, to teach him how to behave toward honest merchants."

So, when they came near him, one of those three men said: "Well, here are the gazelles; now buy one. Here they are, you old hypocrite; you'll feast your eyes on them, but you can't buy them."

But Hamdani, paying no attention to the men, said to Mohadim, "How much for one of your gazelles?

Then another of those men broke in: “You’re very innocent, aren’t you? You know, as well as I do, that gazelles are sold every day at two for a quarter.”

Still taking no notice of these outsiders, Hamdani continued, “I’d like to buy one for a dime.”

“One for a dime!” laughed the men; “of course you’d like to buy one for a dime. Perhaps you’d also like to have the dime to buy with.”

Then one of them gave him a push on the cheek.

At this Hamdani turned and said:

“Why do you push me on the cheek, when I’ve done nothing to you? I do not know you. I call this man, to transact some business with him, and you, who are strangers, step in to spoil our trade.”

He then untied the knot in the corner of his ragged coat, produced the dime, and, handing it to Mohadim, said, “Please, good man, let me have a gazelle for that.”

At this, the countryman took a small gazelle out of the cage and handed it to him, saying, "Here, master, take this one. I call it Kijipaa." Then turning to those three men, he laughed, and said: "Ehe! How's this? You, with your white robes, and turbans, and swords, and daggers, and sandals on your feet-you gentlemen of property, and no mistake you told me this man was too poor to buy anything; yet he has bought a gazelle for a dime, while you fine fellows, I think, haven't enough money among you to buy half a gazelle, if they were five cents each."

Then Mohadim and the three men went their several ways.

As for Hamdani, he stayed at the dust heap until he found a few grains of millet for himself and a few for Kijipaa, the gazelle, and then went to his hut, spread his sleeping mat, and he and the gazelle slept together.

This going to the dust heap for a few grains of millet and then going home to bed continued for about a week.

Then one night Hamdani was awakened by some one calling, "Master! Sitting up, he answered: “Here I am. Who calls?” The gazelle answered, “I do!”

Upon this, the beggar man became so scared that he did not know whether he should faint or get up and run away.

Seeing him so overcome, Kijipaa asked, “Why, master, what’s the matter?

“Oh, gracious!” he gasped; “what a wonder I see!”

“A wonder? said the gazelle, looking all around; “why, what is this wonder, that makes you act as if you were all amazed?”

“Why, it’s so wonderful, I can hardly believe I’m awake!” said his master. “Who in the world ever before knew of a gazelle that could speak?”

“Oho!” laughed Kijipaa; “is that all? There are many more wonderful things than that. But now, listen, while I tell you why I called you.”

“Certainly; I’ll listen to every word,” said the man. I can’t help listening!”

“Well, you see, it’s just this way,” said Kijipaa; “I’ve allowed you to become my master, and I cannot run away from you; so I want you to make an agreement with me, and I will make you a promise, and keep it."

"Say on," said his master.

"Now," continued the gazelle, "one doesn't have to be acquainted with you long, in order to discover that you are very poor. This scratching a few grains of millet from the dust heap every day, and managing to subsist upon them, is all very well for you -you're used to it, because it's a matter of necessity with you; but if I keep it up much longer, you won't have any gazelle - Kijipaa will die of starvation. Therefore, I want to go away every day and feed on my own kind of food; and I promise you I will return every evening."

"Well, I guess I'll have to give my consent," said the man, in no very cheerful tone.

As it was now dawn, Kijipaa jumped up and ran out of the door, Hamdani following him. The gazelle ran very fast, and his master stood watching him until he disappeared. Then tears started in the man's eyes, and, raising his hands, he cried, "Oh, my mother!" Then he cried, "Oh, my father!" Then he cried, "Oh, my gazelle! It has run away!"

Some of his neighbors, who heard him carrying on in this manner, took the opportunity to inform him that he was a fool, an idiot, and a dissipated fellow.

Said one of them: "You hung around that dust heap, goodness knows how long scratching like a hen, till fortune gave you a dime. You hadn't sense enough to go and buy some decent food; you had to buy a gazelle. Now you've let the creature run away. What are you crying about? You brought all your trouble on yourself."

All this, of course, was very comforting to Hamdani who slunk off to the dust heap, got a few grains of millet, and came back to his hut, which now seemed meaner and more desolate than ever.

At sunset, however, Kijipaa came trotting in; and the beggar was happy again, and said, "Ah, my friend, you have returned to me."

"Of course," said the gazelle; "didn't I promise you? You see, I feel that when you bought me you gave all the money you had in the world, even though it was only a dime. Why, then, should I grieve you? I couldn't do it. If I go and get myself some food, I'll always come back evenings."

When the neighbors saw the gazelle come home every evening and run off every morning they were greatly surprised, and began to suspect that Hamdani was a wizard.

Well, this coming and going continued for five days, the gazelle telling its master each night what fine places it had been to, and how much food it had eaten.

On the sixth day it was feeding among some thorn bushes in a thick wood, when, scratching away some bitter grass at the foot of a big tree, it saw an immense diamond of intense brightness.

"Oho!" said Kijipaa, in great astonishment; "here's property, and no mistake! This is worth a kingdom If I take it to my master he will be killed; for, being a poor man, if they say to him, ' Where did you get it?' and he answers, 'I picked it up,' they will not believe him; if he says, 'It was given to me,' they will not believe him either. It will not do for me to get my master into difficulties. I know what I'll do. I'll seek some powerful person; he will use it properly."

So Kijipaa started off through the forest, holding the diamond in his mouth, and ran, and ran, but saw no town that day; so he slept in the forest, and arose at dawn and pursued his way. And the second day passed like the first.

On the third day the gazelle had traveled from dawn until between eight and nine o'clock, when he began to see scattered houses, getting larger in size, and knew he was approaching a town. In due time he found himself in the main street of a large city, leading direct to the sultan's palace, and began to run as fast as he could. People passing along stopped to look at the strange sight of a gazelle running swiftly along the main street with something wrapped in green leaves between its teeth.

The sultan was sitting at the door of his palace, when Kijipaa, stopping a little way off, dropped the diamond from its mouth, and, lying down beside it, panting, called out: "Ho, there! Ho, there!" which is a cry every one makes in that part of the world when wishing to enter a house, remaining outside until the cry is answered.

After the cry had been repeated several times, the sultan said to his attendants; "Who is doing all that calling?"

And one answered, "Master, it's a gazelle that's calling, 'Ho, there!'"

"Ho-ho!" said the sultan; "Ho-ho! Invite the gazelle to, come near."

Then three attendants ran to Kijipaa and said: "Come, get up. The sultan commands you to come near."

So the gazelle arose, picked up the diamond, and, approaching the sultan, laid the jewel at his feet, saying, "Master, good afternoon!" To which the sultan replied: "May God make it good! Come near."

The sultan ordered his attendants to bring a carpet and a large cushion, and desired the gazelle to rest upon them. When it protested that it was comfortable as it was, he insisted, and Keejeepaa had to allow himself to be made a very honored guest. Then they brought milk and rice, and the sultan would hear nothing until the gazelle had fed and rested.

At last, when everything had been disposed

of, the sultan said, "Well, now, my friend, tell me what news you bring."

And Kijipaa said: "Master, I don't exactly know how you will like the news I bring. The fact is, I'm sent here to insult you! I've come to try and pick a quarrel with you! In fact, I'm here to propose a family alliance with you!"

At this the sultan exclaimed: "Oh, come! for a gazelle, you certainly know how to talk! Now, the fact of it is, I'm looking for some one to insult me. I'm just aching to have some one pick a quarrel with me. I'm impatient for a family alliance. Go on with your message."

Then Kijipaa said, "You don't bear any ill will against me, who am only a, messenger?

And the sultan said, "None at all."

"Well," said Kijipaa, "look at this pledge I bring; " dropping the diamond wrapped in leaves into the sultan's lap.

When the sultan opened the leaves and saw the great, sparkling jewel, he was overcome with astonishment. At last he said, "Well?"

"I have brought this pledge," said the gazelle, "from my master, Sultan Darani. He has heard that you have a daughter, so he sent you this jewel, hoping you will forgive him for not sending something more worthy of your acceptance than this trifle."

"Goodness!" said the sultan to himself; "he calls this a trifle" Then to the gazelle: "Oh, that's all right; that's all right. I'm satisfied. The Sultan Darani has my consent to marry my daughter, and I don't want a single thing from him. Let him come empty-handed. If he has more of these trifles, let him leave them at home. This is my message, and I hope you will make it perfectly clear to your master."

The gazelle assured him that he would explain everything satisfactorily, adding, "And now, master, I take my leave. I go straight to our own town, and hope that in about eleven days we shall return to be your guests." So, with mutual compliments, they parted.

In the meantime, Hamdani was having an exceedingly tough time. Kijipaa having disappeared, he wandered about the town moaning, "Oh, my poor gazelle! my poor gazelle!" while the neighbors laughed and jeered at him, until,

Dropping the diamond wrapped in leaves into the sultan's lap

between them and his loss, he was nearly out of his mind.

But one evening, when he had gone to bed, Kijipaa walked in. Up he jumped, and began to embrace the gazelle, and weep over it, and carry on at a great rate.

When he thought there had been about enough of this kind of thing, the gazelle said: "Come, come; keep quiet, my master. I've brought you good news." But the beggar man continued to cry and fondle, and declare that he had thought his gazelle was dead.

At last Kijipaa said: "Oh, well, master, you see I'm all right. You must brace up, and prepare to hear my news, and do as I advise you."

"Go on; go on," replied his master; "explain what you will, I'll do whatever you require me to do. If you were to say, 'Lie down on your back, that I may roll you over the side of the hill,' I would lie down."

"Well," said the gazelle, "there is not much to explain just now, but I'll tell you this: I've seen many kinds of food, food that is desirable and food that is objectionable, but this food I'm about to offer you is very sweet indeed."

"What?" said Hamdani "Is it possible that in this world there is anything that is positively good? There must be good and bad in everything. Food that is both sweet and bitter is good food, but if food were nothing but sweetness, would it not be injurious?"

"H'm!" yawned the gazelle; "I'm too tired to talk philosophy. Let's go to sleep now, and when I call you in the morning, all you have to do is to get up and follow me.

So at dawn they set forth, the gazelle leading the way, and for five days they journeyed through the forest.

On the fifth day they came to a stream, and Keejeepaa said to his master, "Lie down here." When he had done so, the gazelle set to and beat him so soundly that he cried out: "Oh, let up, I beg of you!"

"Now," said the gazelle, "I'm going away, and when I return I expect to find you right here; so don't you leave this spot on any account." Then he ran away, and about ten o'clock that morning he arrived at the house of the sultan.

Now, ever since the day Kijipaa left the town, soldiers had been placed along the road to watch for and announce the approach of Sultan Darani; so one of them, when he saw the gazelle in the distance, rushed up and cried to the sultan, "Sultan Darani is coming! I've seen the gazelle running as fast as it can in this direction."

The sultan and his attendants immediately set out to meet his guests; but when they had gone a little way beyond the town they met the gazelle coming along alone, who, on reaching the Sultan, said, "Good day, my master." The Sultan replied in kind, and asked the news, but Kijipaa said: "Ah, do not ask me. I can scarcely walk, and my news is bad!"

"Why, how is that?" asked the sultan.

"Oh, dear!" sighed the gazelle; "such misfortune and misery! You see, Sultan Darani and I started alone to come here, and we got along all right until we came to the thick part of the forest yonder, when we were met by robbers, who seized my master, bound him, beat him, and took everything he had, even stripping off every stitch of his clothing. Oh, dear! oh, dear!"

"Dear me!" said the sultan we must attend to this at once." So, hurrying back with his attendants to his house, he called a groom, to whom he said, "Saddle the best horse in my stable, and put on him my finest harness." Then he directed a woman servant to open the big inlaid chest and bring him a bag of clothes. When she brought it he picked out a loin-cloth, and a long white robe, and a black overjacket, and a shawl for the waist, and a turban cloth, all of the very finest. Then he sent for a curved sword with a gold hilt, and a curved dagger with gold filigree, and a pair of elegant sandals, and a fine walking-cane.

Then the sultan said to Kijipaa, "Take some of my soldiers, and let them convey these things to Sultan Darani, that he may dress himself and come to me."

But the gazelle answered: "Ah, my master, can I take these soldiers with me and put Sultan Darani to shame? There he lies, beaten and robbed, and I would not have any one see him. I can take everything by myself."

"Why," exclaimed the sultan, "here is a horse, and there are clothes and arms. I don't see how a little gazelle can manage all those things."

But the gazelle had them fasten everything on the horse's back, and tie the end of the bridle around his own neck, and then he set off alone, amidst the wonder and admiration of the people of that city, high and low.

When he arrived at the place where he had left the beggar-man, he found him lying waiting for him, and overjoyed at his return.

"Now," said he, "I have brought you the sweet food I promised. Come, get up and bathe yourself."

With the hesitation of a person long unaccustomed to such a thing, the man stepped into the stream and began to wet himself a little.

"Oh," said the gazelle, impatiently, "a little water like that won't do *you* much good; get out into the deep pool."

"Dear me!" said the man, timidly; there is so much water there; and where there is much water there are sure to be horrible animals."

"Animals! What kind of animals?"

"Well, crocodiles, water lizards, snakes, and, at any rate, frogs; and they bite people, and I'm terribly afraid of all of them."

"Oh, well," said Kijipaa, "do the best you can in the stream; but rub yourself well with earth, and, for goodness' sake, scrub your teeth well with sand; they are awfully dirty."

So the man obeyed, and soon made quite a change in his appearance.

Then the gazelle said: "Here, hurry up and put on these things. The sun has gone down, and we ought to have started before this."

So the man dressed himself in the fine clothes the sultan had sent, and then he mounted the horse, and they started, the gazelle trotting on ahead.

When they had gone some distance, the gazelle stopped, and said, "See here: nobody who sees you now would suspect that you are the man who scratched in the dust heap yesterday. Even if we were to go back to our town the neighbors would not recognize you, if it were only for the fact that your face is clean and your teeth are white. Your appearance is all right, but I have a caution to give you. Over there, where we are going I have procured for you the sultan's daughter for a wife, with all the usual wedding gifts. Now, You must keep quiet. Say nothing except, 'How d'ye do?' and 'What's the news?' Let me do the talking."

"All right," said the man; "that suits me exactly."

"Do you know what your name is"

"Of course I do."

"Indeed? Well, what is it?"

"Why, my name is Hamdani."

"Not at all," laughed Kijipaa; "your name is Sultan Darani."

"Oh, is it?" said his master. That's good."

So they started forward again, and in a little while they saw soldiers running in every direction, and fourteen of these joined them to escort them. Then they saw ahead of them the sultan, and the viziers, and the emirs and the judges, and the great men of the city, coming to meet them.

"Now, then," said Kijipaa, "get off your

horse and salute your father-in-law. That's him in the middle, wearing the sky-blue jacket."

"All right said the man, jumping off his horse, which was then led by a soldier.

So the two met, and the sultans shook hands, and kissed each other, and walked up to the palace together.

Then they had a great feast, and made merry and talked until night, at which time Sultan Darani and the gazelle were put into an inner room, with three soldiers at the door to guard and attend upon them.

When the morning came, Kijipaa went to the sultan and said: "Master, we wish to attend to the business which brought us here. We want to marry your daughter, and the sooner the ceremony takes place, the better it will please the Sultan Darani."

"Why, that's all right," said the sultan; "the bride is ready. Let someone call the teacher, Mwalimu, and tell him to come at once."

When Mwalimu arrived, the sultan said, "See here, we want you to marry this gentleman to my daughter right away."

"All right I'm ready,"said the teacher. So they were married.

Early the next morning the gazelle said to his master: "Now I'm off on a journey. I shall be gone about a week; but however Iong I am gone, don't you leave the house till I return. Good-bye."

Then he went to the real sultan and said: "Good master, Sultan Darani has ordered me to return to our town and put his house in order; he commands me to be here again in a week; if I do not return by that time, he will stay here until come."

The sultan asked him if he would not like to have some soldiers go with him; but the gazelle replied that he was quite competent to take care of himself, as his previous journeys had proved, and he preferred to go alone; so with mutual good wishes they parted.

But Kijipaa did not go in the direction of the old village. He struck off by another road through the forest, and after a time came to a very fine town, of large, handsome houses. As he went through the principal street, right to the far end, he was greatly astonished to observe that the town seemed to have no inhabitants, for he saw neither man, woman, nor child in all the place.

At the end of the main street he came upon the largest and most beautiful house he had ever seen, built of sapphire, and turquoise, and costly marbles.

"Oh, my!" said the gazelle; "this house would just suit my master. I'll have to pluck up my courage and see whether this is deserted like the other houses in this mysterious town."

So Kijipaa knocked at the door, and called, "Hullo, there!" several times; but no one answered. And he said to himself: "This is strange! If there were no one inside, the door would be fastened on the outside. Perhaps they are in another part of the house, or asleep. I'll call again, louder."

So he called again, very loud and long, "Hullo, th-e-re! Hul-lo!" And directly an old woman inside answered," Who is that calling so loudly?"

"It is I, your grandchild, good mistress," said Kijipaa.

"If you are my grandchild," replied the old woman, "go back to your home at once; don't come and die here, and bring me to my death also."

"Oh, come," said he, "open the door, mistress; I have just a few words I wish to say to you."

"My dear grandson," she replied, "the only reason why I do not open the door is because I fear to endanger both your life and my own."

"Oh, don't worry about that; I guess your life and mine are safe enough for a while. Open the door, anyhow, and hear the little I have to say."

So the old woman opened the door.

Then they exchanged salutations and compliments, after which she asked the gazelle, "What's the news from your place, grandson?"

"Oh, everything is going along pretty well," said he; "what's the news around here?"

"All the news here is very bad," sighed the old creature. If you're looking for a place to die in, you've struck it here. I've not the slightest doubt you'll see all you want of death this very day."

"Hub!" replied Kijipaa, lightly; "for a fly to die in honey is not bad for the fly, and doesn't injure the honey."

"It may be all very well for you to be easy about it," persisted the old person; but if people with swords and shields did not escape, how can a little thing like you avoid danger? I must again beg of you to go back to the place you came from. Your safety seems of more interest to me than it is to you."

"Well, you see, I can't go back just now; and besides, I want to find out more about this place. Who owns it?"

"Ah, grandson, in this house are enormous wealth, numbers of people, hundreds of horses, and the owner is Nyoka Mkuu, the wonderfully big snake. He owns this whole town, also."

"Oho! Is that so? "said Kijipaa. Look here, old lady; can't you put me on to some plan of getting near this big snake, that I may kill him?"

"Mercy!" cried the old woman, in affright; "don't talk like that. You've put my life in danger already, for I'm sure Nyoka Mkuu can hear what is said in this house, wherever he is. You see, I'm a poor old woman, and I have been placed here, with those pots and pans, to cook for him. Well, when the big snake is coming, the wind begins to blow and the dust flies as it would do in a great storm. Then, when he arrives in the courtyard, he eats until he is full, and after that, goes inside there to drink water. When he has finished, he goes away again. This occurs every other day, just when the sun is overhead. I may add that Nyoka Mkuu has seven heads. Now, then, do you think yourself a match for him?"

"Look here, mother," said the gazelle, "don't you worry about, me. Has this big snake a sword?"

"He has. This is it," said she, taking from its peg a very keen and beautiful blade, and handing it to him; "but what's the use in bothering about it? We are dead already."

"We shall see about that," said Kijipaa.

Just at that moment the wind began to blow, and the dust to fly, as if a great storm were approaching.

"Do you hear the great one coming?" cried the old woman.

"Pshaw!" said the gazelle; "I'm a great one also and I have the advantage of being on the inside. Two bulls can't live in one cattle-pen. Either he will live in this house, or I will."

Notwithstanding the terror the old lady was in, she had to smile at the assurance of this little undersized gazelle, and repeated over again her account of the people with swords and shields who had been killed by the big snake.

"Ah, stop your gabbling," said the gazelle; "you can't always judge a banana by its color or size. Wait and see, grandma."

In a very little while the big snake, Nyoka Mkuu, came into the courtyard, and went around to all the pots and ate their contents. Then he came to the door.

"Hullo, old lady," said he; "how is it I smell a new kind of odor inside there?"

"Oh, that's nothing, good master," replied the old woman; "I've been so busy around here lately I haven't had time to look after myself; but this morning, I used some perfume, and that's what you smell."

Now, Kijipaa had drawn the sword, and was standing just inside the doorway; so, when the big snake put his head in, it was cut off so quickly that its owner did not know it was gone. When he put in his second head it was cut off with the same quickness; and, feeling a little irritation, he exclaimed, "Who's inside there, scratching me?" He then thrust in his third head, and that was cut off also.

This continued until six heads had been disposed of, when Nyoka Mkuu unfolded his rings and lashed around so that the gazelle and the old woman could not see one another through the dust.

Then the snake thrust in his seventh head, and the gazelle, crying: "Now your time has come; you've climbed many trees, but this you cannot climb," severed it, and immediately fell down in a fainting fit.

Well, that old woman, although she was seventy-five years of age, jumped, and shouted, and laughed, like a girl of nine. Then she ran and got water, and sprinkled the gazelle, and turned him this way and that way, until at last he sneezed; which greatly pleased the old person, who fanned him and tended him until he was quite recovered.

"Oh, my!" said she; "who would have thought you could be a match for him, my grandson?"

"Well, well," said Kijipaa; "that's all over. Now show me everything around this place."

So she showed him everything, from top to bottom: store-rooms full of goods, chambers full of expensive foods, rooms containing handsome people who had been kept prisoners for a long time, slaves, and everything.

Next he asked her if there was any person who was likely to lay claim to the place or make any trouble; and she answered: "No one; everything here belongs to you."

"Very well, then," said he, "you stay here and take care of these things until I bring my master. This place belongs to him now."

Kijipaa stayed three days examining the house, and said to himself: "Well, when my master comes here he will be much pleased with what I have done for him, and he'll appreciate it after the life he's been accustomed to. As for his father-in-law, there is not a house in his town that can compare with this."

On the fourth day he departed, and in due time arrived at the town where the sultan and his master lived. Then there were great rejoicings; the sultan being particularly pleased at his return, while his master felt as if he had received a new lease of life.

After everything had settled down a little, Kijipaa told his master he must be ready to go, with his wife, to his new home, after four days. Then he went and told the sultan that Sultan Darani desired to take his wife to his own town in four days; to which the sultan strongly objected; but the gazelle said it was his master's wish, and at last everything was arranged.

On the day of the departure a great company assembled to escort Sultan Darani and his bride. There were the bride's ladies-in-waiting, and slaves, and horsemen, and Kijipaa leading them all.

So they traveled three days, resting when

the sun was overhead, and stopping each evening about five o'clock to eat and sleep; arising next morning at daybreak, eating, and going forward again. And all this time the gazelle took very little rest, going all through the company, from the ladies to the slaves, and seeing that every one was well supplied with food and quite comfortable; therefore the entire company loved him and valued him like the apples of their eyes.

On the fourth day, during the afternoon, many houses came into view, and some of the folks called Kijipaa's attention to them. "Certainly," said he; "that is our town, and that house you see yonder is the palace of Sultan Darani."

So they went on, and all the company filed into the courtyard, while the gazelle and his master went into the house.

When the old woman saw Kijipaa, she began to dance, and shout, and carry on, just as she did when he killed Nyoka Mkuu, and taking up his foot she kissed it; but Kijipaa said: "Old lady, let me alone; the one to be made much of is this my master, Sultan Darani. Kiss his feet; he has the first honors whenever he is present."

The old woman excused herself for not knowing the master, and then Sultan Darani and the gazelle went around on a tour of inspection. The sultan ordered all the prisoners to be released, the horses to be sent out to pasture, all the rooms to be swept, the furniture to be dusted, and, in the meantime, servants were busy preparing food. Then every one had apartments assigned to him, and all were satisfied.

After they had remained there some time, the ladies who had accompanied the bride expressed a desire to return to their own homes. Kijipaa begged them not to hurry away, but after a while they departed, each loaded with gifts by the gazelle, for whom they had a thousand times more affection than for his master. Then things settled down to their regular routine.

One day the gazelle said to the old woman: "I think the conduct of my master is very singular. I have done nothing but good for him all the time I have been with him. I came to this town and braved many dangers for him, and when all was over I gave everything to him. Yet be has never asked: 'How did you get this house? How did you get this town? Who is the owner of this house? Have you rented all these things, or have they been given you? What has become of the inhabitants of the place?' I don't understand him. And further: although I have done nothing but good for him, he has never done one good thing for me. Nothing here is really his. He never saw such a house or town as this since the day he was born, and he doesn't own anything of it. I believe the old folks were right when they said, 'If you want to do any person good, don't do too much; do him a little harm occasionally, and he'll think more of you.' However, I've done all I can now, and I'd like' to see him make some little return."

Next morning the old woman was awakened early by the gazelle calling, "Mother! Mother!" When she went to him she found he was sick in his stomach, feverish, and all his legs ached.

"Go," said he, "and tell my master I am very ill."

So she went upstairs and found the master and mistress sitting on a marble couch, covered with a striped silk scarf from India.

"Well," said the master, "what do you want, old woman?"

"Oh, my master," cried she, "Kijipaa is sick!"

The mistress started and said: "Dear me! What is the matter with him?"

"All his body pains him. He is sick all over."

"Oh, well," said the master, "what can I do? Go and get some of that red millet, that is too common for our use, and make him some gruel."

"Gracious!" explaimed his wife, staring at him in amazement; "do you wish her to feed our friend with stuff that a horse would not eat if he were ever so hungry? This is not right of you."

"Ah, get out!" said he, "you're crazy. We eat rice; isn't red millet good enough for a gazelle that cost only a dime?"

"Oh, but he is no ordinary gazelle. He should be as dear to you as the apple of your eye. If sand got in your eye it would trouble you."

"You talk too much," returned her husband; then, turning to the old woman, he said, "Go and do as I told you."

So the old woman went downstairs, and when she saw the gazelle, she began to cry, and say, "Oh, dear! oh, dear!"

It was a long while before the gazelle could persuade her to tell him what had passed upstairs, but at last she told him all. When he had heard it, he said: "Did he really tell you to make me red millet gruel?"

"Ah," cried she, "do you think I would say such a thing if it were not so?"

"Well," said Kijipaa, "I believe what the old folks said was right. However, we'll give him another chance. Go up to him again, and tell him I am very sick, and that I can't eat that gruel."

So she went upstairs, and found the master and mistress sitting by the window, drinking coffee.

The master, looking around and seeing her, said: "What's the matter now, old woman?"

And she said: "Master, I am sent by Kijipaa. He is very sick indeed, and has not taken the gruel you told me to make for him."

"Oh, bother!" he exclaimed. "Hold your

tongue, and keep your feet still, and shut your eyes, and stop your ears with wax; then, if that gazelle tells you to come up here, say that your legs are stiff; and if he tells you to listen, say your ears are deaf; and if he tells you to look, say your sight has failed you; and if he wants you to talk, tell him your tongue is paralyzed."

When the old woman heard these words, she stood and stared, and was unable to move. As for his wife, her face became sad, and the tears began to start from her eyes; observing which, her husband said, sharply, "What's the matter with you, sultan's daughter?"

The lady replied, "A man's madness is his undoing."

"Why do you say that, mistress?" he inquired.

"Ah," said she, "I am grieved, my husband, at your treatment of Kijipaa. Whenever I say a good word for the gazelle you dislike to hear it. I pity you that your understanding is gone."

"What do you mean by talking in that manner to me?" he blustered.

"Why, advice is a blessing, if properly taken.

A husband should advise with his wife, and a wife with her husband; then they are both blessed."

"Oh, stop," said her husband, impatiently; "it's evident you've lost your senses. You should be chained up." Then he said to the old woman: "Never mind her talk and as to this gazelle, tell him to stop bothering me and putting on style, as if he were the sultan. I can't eat, I can't drink, I can't sleep, because of that gazelle worrying me with his messages. First, the gazelle is sick; then, the gazelle doesn't like what he gets to eat. Confound it! If he likes to eat, let him eat; if he doesn't like to eat, let him die and be out of the way. My mother is dead, and my father is dead, and I still live and eat; shall I be put out of my way by a gazelle, that I bought for a dime, telling me he wants this thing or that thing? Go and tell him to learn how to behave himself toward his superiors."

When the old woman went downstairs, she found the gazelle was bleeding at the mouth, and in a very bad way. All she could say was, "My son, the good you did is all lost; but be patient."

And the gazelle wept with the old woman when she told him all that had passed, and he said, "Mother, I am dying, not only from sickness, but from shame and anger at this man's ingratitude."

After a while Kijipaa told the old woman to go and tell the master that he believed he was dying. When she went upstairs she found Darani chewing sugar-cane, and she said to him, "Master, the gazelle is worse; we think him nearer to dying than getting well."

To which he answered: "Haven't I told you often enough not to bother me?"

Then his wife said: "Oh, husband, won't you go down and see the poor gazelle? If you don't like to go, let me go and see him. He never gets a single good thing from you."

But he turned to the old woman and said, "Go and tell that nuisance of a gazelle to die eleven times if he chooses to."

"Now, husband," persisted the lady, "what has Kijipaa done to you? Has he done you any wrong? Such words as yours people use to their enemies only. Surely the gazelle is not your enemy. All the people who know him, great and lowly, love him dearly, and they will think it very wrong of you if you neglect him. Now, do be kind to him, Sultan Darani."

But he only repeated his assertion that she had lost her wits, and would have nothing further of argument.

So the old woman went down and found the gazelle worse than ever.

In the meantime Sultan Darani's wife managed to give some rice to a servant to cook for the gazelle, and also sent him a soft shawl to cover him and a pillow to lie upon. She also sent him a message that if he wished, she would have her father's best physicians attend him.

All this was too late, however, for just as these good things arrived, Kijipaa died.

When the people heard he was dead, they went running around crying and having an awful time; and when Sultan Darani found out what all the commotion was about he was very indignant, remarking, "Why, you are making as much fuss as if I were dead, and all over a gazelle that I bought for a dime!"

But his wife said: "Husband, it was this gazelle that came to ask me of my father, it was be who brought me from my father's, and it was to him I was given by my father. He gave you everything good, and you do not possess a thing that he did not procure for you. He did everything he could to help you, and you not only returned him unkindness, but now he is dead you have ordered people to throw him into the well. Let us alone, that we may weep."

But the gazelle was taken and thrown into the well.

Then the lady wrote a letter telling her father to come to her directly, and despatched it by trusty messengers; upon the receipt of which the sultan and his attendants started hurriedly to visit his daughter.

When they arrived, and heard that the gazelle was dead and had been thrown into the well, they wept very much; and the sultan, and the vizier, and the judges, and the rich chief men, all went down into the well and brought up the body of Kijipaa, and took it away with them and buried it.

Now, that night the lady dreamt that she was at home at her father's house; and when dawn came she awoke and found she was in her own bed in her own town again.

And her husband dreamed that he was on the dust heap, scratching; and when he awoke there he was, with both hands full of dust, looking for grains of millet. Staring wildly he looked around to the right and left, saying: "Oh, who has played this trick on me? How did I get back here, I wonder?"

Just then the children going along, and seeing him, laughed and hooted at him, calling out: "Hello, Hamdani, where have you been? Where do you come from? We thought you were dead long ago."

So the sultan's daughter lived in happiness with her people until the end, and that beggarman continued to scratch for grains of millet in the dust heap until he died.

If this story is good, the goodness belongs to all; if it is bad, the badness belongs only to him who told it.

The gazelle wept with the old woman

VIII
MKAA JIKONI, THE BOY HUNTER

Sultan Majnun had seven sons and a big cat, of all of whom he was very proud.

Everything went well until one day the cat went and caught a calf. When they told the sultan he said, "Well, the cat is mine, and the calf is mine." So they said, "Oh, all right, master," and let the matter drop.

A few days later the cat caught a goat; and when they told the sultan he said, "The cat is mine, and the goat is mine;" and so that settled it again.

Two days more passed, and the cat caught a cow. They told the sultan, and he shut them up with "My cat, and my cow."

After another two days the cat caught a donkey; same result.

Next it caught a horse; same result.

The next victim was a camel; and when they told the sultan he said: “What’s the matter with you folks? It was my cat, and my camel. I believe you don’t like my cat, and want it killed, bringing me tales about it every day. Let it eat whatever it wants to.”

In a very short time it caught a child, and then a full-grown man; but each time the sultan remarked that both the cat and its victim were his, and thought no more of it.

Meantime the cat grew bolder, and hung around a low, open place near the town, pouncing on people going for water, or animals out at pasture, and eating them.

At last some of the people plucked up courage; and, going to the sultan, said: “How is this, master? As you are our sultan you are our protector, - or ought to be, - yet you have allowed this cat to do as it pleases, and now it lives just out of town there, and kills everything living that goes that way, while at night it comes into town and does the same thing. Now, what on earth are we to do?”

But Majnun only replied: “I really believe

They crept cautiously through the bushes

you hate my cat. I suppose you want me to kill it; but I shall do no such thing. Everything it eats is mine."

Of course the folks were astonished at this result of the interview, and, as no one dared to kill the cat, they all had to remove from the vicinity where it lived. But this did not mend matters, because, when it found no one came that way, it shifted its quarters likewise.

So complaints continued to pour in, until at last Sultan Majnun gave orders that if any one came to make accusations against the cat, he was to be informed that the master could not be seen.

When things got so that people neither let their animals out nor went out themselves, the cat went farther into the country, killing and eating cattle, and fowls, and everything that came its way.

One day the sultan said to six of his sons, "I'm going to look at the country to-day; come along with me."

The seventh son was considered too young to go around anywhere, and was always left at

They camped for the night

home with the women folk, being called by his brothers Mkaa Jikoni, which means Mr. Sit-in-the-kitchen.

Well, they went, and presently came to a thicket. The father was in front and the six sons following him, when the cat jumped out and killed three of the latter.

The attendants shouted, "The cat! the cat!" and the soldiers asked permission to search for and kill it, which the sultan readily granted, saying: "This is not a cat, it is a Nunda. It has taken from me my own sons."

Now, nobody had ever seen a nunda, but they all knew it was a terrible beast that could kill and eat all other living things.

When the sultan began to bemoan the loss of his sons, some of those who heard him said: "Ah, master, this Nunda does not select his prey. He doesn't say: 'This is my master's son, I'll leave him alone,' or, 'This is my master's wife, I won't eat her. When we told you what the cat had done, you always said it was your cat, and what it ate was yours, and now it has killed your sons, and we don't believe it would hesitate to eat even you."

And he said, "I fear you are right."

As for the soldiers who tried to get the cat, some were killed and the remainder ran away, and the sultan and his living sons took the dead bodies home and buried them.

Now when Mkaa Jikoni, the seventh son, heard that his brothers had been killed by the Nunda, he said to his mother, "I, too, will go, that it may kill me as well as my brothers, or I will kill it."

But his mother said: "My son, I do not like to have you go. Those three are already dead; and if you are killed also, will not that be one wound upon another to my heart?"

"Nevertheless," said he, "I cannot help going; but do not tell my father."

So his mother made him some cakes, and sent some attendants with him; and he took a great spear, as sharp as a razor, and a sword, bade her farewell, and departed.

As he had always been left at home, he had no very clear idea what he was going to hunt for; so he had not gone far beyond the suburbs, when, seeing a very large dog, he concluded that this was the animal he was after; so he killed it, tied a rope to it, and dragged it home, singing,

"Oh, mother, I have killed
The Nunda, eater of the people."

When his mother, who was upstairs,heard him, she looked out of the window, and, seeing what he had brought, said, "My son, this is not the Nunda, eater of the people."

So he left the carcass outside and went in to talk about it, and his mother said, "My dear boy, the Nunda is a much larger animal than that; but if I were you, I'd give the business up and stay at home."

"No, indeed," he exclaimed; "no staying at home for me until I have met and fought the Nunda."

So he set out again, and went a great deal farther than he had gone on the former day. Presently he saw a civet cat, and, believing it to be the animal he was in search of, he-killed it, bound it, and dragged it home, singing,

"Oh, mother, I have killed
The Nunda, eater of the people."

When his mother saw the civet cat, she said, "My son, this is not the Nunda, eater of the people." And he threw it away.

Again his mother entreated him to stay at home, but he would not listen to her, and started off again.

This time he went away off into the forest, and seeing a bigger cat than the last one, he killed it, bound it, and dragged it home, singing,

"Oh, mother, I have killed
The Nunda, eater of the people."

But directly his mother saw it, she had to tell him, as before, "My son, this is not the nunda, eater of the people."

He was, of course, very much troubled at this; and his mother said, "Now, where do you expect to find this Nunda? You don't know where it is, and you don't know what it looks like. You'll get sick over this; you're not looking so well now as you did. Come, stay at home."

But he said: "There are three things, one of which I shall do: I shall die; I shall find the Nunda and kill it; or I shall return home unsuccessful. In any case, I'm off again."

This time he went farther than before, saw a zebra, killed it, bound it, and dragged it home, singing,

"Oh, mother, I have killed
The Nunda, eater of the people."

Of course his mother had to tell him, once again, "My son, this is not the Nunda, eater of the people."

After a good deal of argument, in which his mother's persuasion, as usual, was of no avail, he went off again, going farther than ever, when he caught a giraffe; and when he had killed it he said: Well, this time I've been successful. This must be the Nunda." So he dragged it home, singing,

"Oh, mother, I have killed
The Nunda, eater of the people."

Again his mother had to assure him, "My son, this is not the Nunda, eater of the people." She then pointed out to him that his brothers were not running about hunting, for the Nunda, but staying at home attending, to their own business. But, remarking that all brothers were not alike, he expressed his determination to stick to his task until it came to a successful termination, and went off again, a still greater distance than before.

While going, through the wilderness he espied a rhinoceros asleep under a tree, and turning to his attendants he exclaimed, "At last I see the Nunda."

"Where, master?" they all cried, eagerly.

"There, under the tree."

"Oh-h! What shall we do?" they asked.

And he answered: "First of all, let us eat our fill, then we will attack it. We have found it in a good place, though if it kills us, we can't help it."

So they all took out their arrowroot cakes and ate till they were satisfied.

Then Mkaa Jikoni said, "Each of you take two guns; lay one beside you and take the other in your hands, and at the proper time let us all fire at once."

And they said, "All right, master."

So they crept cautiously through the bushes and got around to the other side of the tree, at the back of the rhinoceros; then they closed up till they were quite near it, and all fired together. The beast jumped up, ran a little way, and then fell down dead.

They bound it, and dragged it for two whole days, until they reached the town, when Mkaa Jikoni began singing,

"Oh, mother, I have killed
The Nunda, eater of the people."

But he received the same answer from his mother: "My son, this is not the Nunda, eater of the people."

And many persons came and looked at the rhinoceros, and felt very sorry for the young man. As for his father and mother, they both begged of him to give up, his father offering to give him anything he possessed if he would only stay at home. But he said, "I don't hear what you are saying; good-bye," and was off again.

This time he still further increased the distance from his home, and at last he saw an elephant asleep at noon in the forest. Thereupon he said to his attendants, "Now we *have* found the Nunda."

"Ah, where is he?" said they.

"Yonder, in the shade. Do you see it?"

"Oh, yes, master; shall we march up to it?"

"If we march up to it, and it is looking this way, it will come at us, and if it does that, some of us will be killed. I think we had best let one man steal up close and see which way its face is turned."

As every one thought this was a good idea, a slave named Kiroboto crept on his hands and knees, and had a good look at it. When he returned in the same manner, his master asked: "Well, what's the news? Is it the Nunda?"

"I do not know," replied Kiroboto; but I think there is very little doubt that it is. It is broad, with a very big head, and, goodness, I never saw such large ears!"

"All right," said Mkaa Jikoni; let us eat, and then go for it."

So they took their arrowroot cakes, and their molasses cakes, and ate until they were quite full.

Then the youth said to them: "My people, to-day is perhaps the last we shall ever see; so we will take leave of each other. Those who are to escape will escape, and those who are to die will die; but if I die, let those who escape tell my mother and father not to grieve for me."

But his attendants said, "Oh, come along, master; none of us will die, please God."

So they went on their hands and knees till they were close up, and then they said to Mkaa Jikoni, "Give us your plan, master;" but he said, "There is no plan, only let all fire at once."

Well, they fired all at once, and immediately the elephant jumped up and charged at them.

Then such a helter-skelter flight as there was! They threw away their guns and everything they carried, and made for the trees, which they climbed with surprising alacrity.

As to the elephant, he kept straight ahead until he fell down some distance away. They all remained in the trees from three until six o'clock in the morning, without food and without clothing.

The young man sat in his tree and wept bitterly, saying, "I don't exactly know what death is, but it seems to me this must be very like it."

As no one could see any one else, he did not know where his attendants were, and though he wished to come down from the tree, he thought, "Maybe the Nunda is down below there, and will eat me."

Each attendant was in exactly the same fix, wishing to come down, but afraid the Nunda was waiting to eat him.

Kiroboto had seen the elephant fall, but was afraid to get down by himself, saying, "Perhaps, though it has fallen down, it is not dead." But presently he saw a dog go up to it and smell it, and then he was sure it was dead. Then he got down from the tree as fast as he could and gave a signal cry, which was answered; but not being sure from whence the answer came, he repeated the cry, listening intently. When it was answered he went straight to the place from which the sound proceeded, and found two of his companions in one tree. To them he said, "Come on; get down; the Nunda is dead." So they got down quickly and hunted around until they found their master. When they told him the news, he came down also; and after a little the attendants had all gathered together and had picked up their guns and their clothes, and were all right again. But they were all weak and hungry, so they rested and ate some food, after which they went to examine their prize.

As soon as Mkaa Jikoni saw it he said, "Ah, this is the Nunda! This is it! This is it!" And they all agreed that it was it.

So they dragged the elephant three days to their town, and then the youth began singing,

"Oh, mother, this is he,
The Nunda, eater of the people."

He was, naturally, quite upset when his mother replied, "My son, this is not the Nunda, eater of the people." She further said: "Poor boy! what trouble you have been through. All the people are astonished that one so young should have such a great understanding.!"

Then his father and mother began their entreaties again, and finally it was agreed that this next up should be his last, whatever the result might be.

Well, they started off again, and went on and on, past the forest, until they came to a very high mountain, at the foot of which they camped for the night.

In the morning they cooked their rice and ate it, and then Mkaa Jikoni said: "Let us now climb the mountain, and look all over the country from its peak." And they went and they went, until after a long, weary while, they reached the top, where they sat down to rest and form their plans.

Now, one of the attendants, named Shindano, while walking about, cast his eyes down the side of the mountain, and suddenly saw a great beast about half way down; but he could not make out its appearance distinctly, on account of the distance and the trees. Calling his master, he pointed it out to him, and something in Mkaa Jikoni's heart told him that it was the nunda. To make sure, however, he took his gun and his spear and went partly down the mountain to get a better view.

"Ah," said he, "this must be the Nunda. My mother told me its ears were small, and those are small; she told me the Nunda is broad and short, and so is this; she said it has two blotches, like a civet cat, and there are the blotches; she told me the tall is thick, and there is a thick tail. It must be the Nunda."

Then he went back to his attendants and bade them eat heartily, which they did. Next he told them to leave every unnecessary thing behind, because if they had to run they would be better without encumbrance, and if they were victorious they could return for their goods.

When they had made all their arrangements they started down the mountain, but when they had got about half way down Kiroboto and Shindano were afraid. Then the youth said to them: "Oh, let's go on; don't be afraid. We all have to live and die. What are you frightened about?" So, thus encouraged, they went on.

When they came near the place, Mkaa Jikoni ordered them to take off all their clothing except one piece, and to place that tightly on their bodies, so that if they had to run they would not be caught by thorns or branches.

So when they came close to the beast, they saw that it was asleep, and all agreed that it was the Nunda.

Then the young man said, "Now the sun is setting, shall we fire at it, or let be till morning?"

And they all wished to fire at once, and see what the result would be without further tax on their nerves; therefore they arranged that they should all fire together.

They all crept up close, and when the master gave the word, they discharged their guns together. The nunda did not move; that one dose bad been sufficient. Nevertheless, they all turned and scampered up to the top of the mountain. There they ate and rested for the night.

In the morning they ate their rice, and then went down to see how matters were, when they found the beast lying dead.

After resting and eating, they started homeward, dragging the dead beast with them. On the fourth day it began to give indications of decay, and the attendants wished to abandon it; but Mkaa Jikoni said they would continue to drag it if there was only one bone left.

When they came near the town he began to sing,

"Mother, mother, I have come
From the evil spirits, home.
Mother, listen while I sing;
While I tell you what I bring.
Oh, mother, I have killed
The Nunda, eater of the people."

And when his mother looked out, she cried, "My son, this is the Nunda, eater of the people."

Then all the people came out to welcome him, and his father was overcome with joy, and loaded him with honors, and procured him a rich and beautiful wife; and when he died Mkaa Jikoni became sultan, and lived long and happily, beloved by all the people.

IX
THE MAGICIAN AND THE SULTAN'S SON

There was once a sultan who had three little sons, and no one seemed to be able to teach them anything; which greatly grieved both the sultan and his wife.

One day a magician came to the sultan and said, "If I take your three boys and teach them to read and write, and make great scholars of them, what will you give me?"

And the sultan said, "I will give you half of my property."

"No," said the magician; "that won't do."

I'll give you half of the towns I own." No; that will not satisfy me."

"What do you want, then?"

"When I have made them scholars and bring them back to you, choose two of them for yourself and give me the third; for I want to have a companion of my own.

"Agreed," said the sultan.

So the magician took them away, and in a remarkably short time taught them to read, and to make letters, and made them quite good scholars. Then he took them back to the sultan and said: "Here are the children. They are all equally good scholars. Choose."

So the sultan took the two he preferred, and the magician went away with the third, whose name was Kijana, to his own house, which was a very large one.

When they arrived, Mchawi, the magician, gave the youth all the keys, saying, "Open whatever you wish to." Then he told him that he was his father, and that he was going away for a month.

When he was gone, Kijana took the keys and went to examine the house. He opened one door, and saw a room full of liquid gold. He put his finger in, and the gold stuck to it, and, wipe and rub as he would, the gold would not come off; so he wrapped a piece of rag around it, and when his supposed father came home and saw the rag, and asked him what he had been doing to his finger, he was afraid to tell him the truth, so he said that he had cut it.

Not very long after, Mchawi went away again, and the youth took the keys and continued his investigations.

The first room he opened was filled with the bones of goats, the next with sheep's bones, the next with the bones of oxen, the fourth with the bones of donkeys, the fifth with those of horses, the sixth contained men's skulls, and in the seventh was a live horse.

"Hullo!" said the horse; "where do you come from, you son of Adam?"

"This is my father's house," said Kijana.

"Oh, indeed!" was the reply. Well, you've got a pretty nice parent! Do you know that he occupies himself with eating people, and donkeys, and horses, and oxen and goats and everything he can lay his hands on? You and I are the only living things left."

This scared the youth pretty badly, and he faltered, "What are we to do?"

"What's your name?" said the horse.

"Kijana."

"Well, I'm Farasi. Now, Kijana, first of all, come and unfasten me."

The youth did so at once.

"Now, then, open the door of the room with the gold in it, and I will swallow it all; then I'll go and wait for you under the big tree down the road a little way. When the magician comes home, he will say to you, 'Let us go for firewood;' then you answer, 'I don't understand that work;' and he will go by himself. When he comes back, he will put a great big pot on the hook and will tell you to make a fire under it. Tell him you don't know how to make a fire, and he will make it himself.

"Then he will bring a large quantity of butter, and while it is getting hot he will put up a swing and say to you, 'Get up there, and I'll swing you.' But you tell him you never played at that game, and ask him to swing first, that you may see how it is done. Then he will get up to show you; and you must push him into the big pot, and then come to me as quickly as you can."

Then the horse went away.

Now, Mchawi had invited some of his friends to a feast at his house that evening; so, returning home early, he said to Kijana, "Let us go for firewood;" but the youth answered, "I don't understand that work." So he went by himself and brought the wood.

Then he hung up the big pot and said, "Light the fire;" but the youth said, "I don't know how to do it." So the magician laid the wood under the pot and lighted it himself.

Then he said, "Put all that butter in the pot;" but the youth answered, I can't lift it; I'm not strong enough." So he put in the butter himself.

Next Mchawi said, "Have you seen our country game?" And Kijana answered, "I think not."

"Well," said the magician "let's play at it while the butter is getting hot."

So he tied up the swing and said to Kijana, "Get up here, and learn the game." But the youth said: "You get up first and show me. I'll learn quicker that way."

The magician got into the swing, and just as he got started Kijana gave him a push right into the big pot; and as the butter was by this time boiling, it not only killed him, but cooked him also.

As soon as the youth had pushed the magician into the big pot, he ran as fast as he could to the big tree, where the horse was waiting for him.

"Come on," said Farasi; "jump on my back and let's be going."

So he mounted and they started off.

When the magician's guests arrived they looked everywhere for him, but, of course, could not find him. Then, after waiting a while, they began to be very hungry; so, looking around for something to eat, they saw that the stew in the big pot was done, and, saying to each other, "Let's begin, anyway," they started in and ate the entire contents of the pot. After they had finished, they searched for Mchawi again, and finding lots of provisions in the house, they thought they would stay there until he came; but after they had waited a couple of days and

The magician gave the youth all the keys

eaten all the food in the place, they gave him up and returned to their homes.

Meanwhile Kijana and the horse continued on their way until they had gone a great distance, and at last they stopped near a large town.

"Let us stay here," said the youth, "and build a house."

As Farasi was agreeable, they did so. The horse coughed up all the gold he had swallowed, with which they purchased slaves, and cattle, and everything they needed.

When the people of the town saw the beautiful new house and all the slaves, and cattle, and riches it contained, they went and told their sultan, who at once made up his mind that the owner of such a place must be of sufficient importance to be visited and taken notice of, as an acquisition to the neighborhood.

So he called on Kijana, and inquired who he was.

"Oh, I'm just an ordinary being, like other people."

"Are you a traveler?

"Well, I have been; but I like this place, and

Right into the big pot!

think I'll settle down here."

"Why don't you come and walk in our town?"

"I should like to very much, but I need some one to show me around."

"Oh, I'll show you around," said the sultan, eagerly, for he was quite taken with the young man.

After this Kijana and the sultan became great friends; and in the course of time the young man married the sultan's daughter, and they had one son.

They lived very happily together, and Kijana loved Farasi as his own soul.

X
THE PHYSICIAN'S SON AND THE KING OF THE SNAKES

Once there was a very learned physician, who died leaving his wife with a little baby boy, whom, when he was old enough, she named, according to his father's wish, Hassibu Karim Ed Din.

When the boy had been to school, and had learned to read, his mother sent him to a tailor, to learn his trade, but he could not learn it. Then he was sent to a silversmith, but he could not learn his trade either. After that he tried many trades, but could learn none of them. At last his mother said, "Well, stay at home for a while;" and that seemed to suit him.

One day he asked his mother what his father's business had been, and she told him he was a very great physician.

"Where are his books?" he asked.

"Well, it's a long time since I saw them," replied his mother, "but I think they are behind there. Look and see."

So he hunted around a little and at last found them, but they are almost ruined by insects, and he gained little from them.

At last, four of the neighbors came to his mother and said, "Let your boy go along with us and cut wood in the forest." It was their business to cut wood, load it on donkey, and sell it in the town for making fires.

"All right," said she; "to-morrow I'll buy him a donkey, and he can start fair with you."

So the next day Hassibu, with his donkey, went off with those four persons, and they worked very hard and made a lot of money that day. This continued for six days, but on the seventh day it rained heavily, and they had to get under the rocks to keep dry.

Now, Hassibu sat in a place by himself, and, having nothing else to do, he picked up a stone and began knocking on the ground with it. To his surprise the ground gave forth a hollow sound, and he called to his companions, saying,

"There seems to be a hole under here."

Upon hearing him knock again, they decided to dig and see what was the cause of the hollow sound; and they had not gone very deep before they broke into a large pit, like a well, which was filled to the top with honey.

They didn't do any firewood chopping after that, but devoted their entire attention to the collection and sale of the honey.

With a view to getting it all out as quickly as possible, they told Hassibu to go down into the pit and dip out the honey, while they put it in vessels and took it to town for sale. They worked for three days, making a great deal of money.

At last there was only a little honey left at the very bottom of the pit, and they told the boy to scrape that together while they went to get a rope to haul him out.

But instead of getting the rope, they decided to let him remain in the pit, and divide the money among themselves. So, when he had gathered the remainder of the honey together, and called for the rope, he received no answer; and after he had been alone in the pit for three days he became convinced that his companions had deserted him.

Then those four persons went to his mother and told her that they had become separated in the forest, that they had heard a lion roaring, and that they could find no trace of either her son or his donkey.

His mother, of course, cried very much, and the four neighbors pocketed her son's share of the money.

To return to Hassibu.

He passed the time walking about the pit, wondering what the end would be, eating scraps of honey, sleeping a little, and sitting down to think.

While engaged in the last occupation, on the fourth day, he saw a scorpion fall to the ground - a large one, too - and he killed it.

Then suddenly he thought to himself, "Where did that scorpion come from? There must be a hole somewhere. I'll search, anyhow."

So he searched around until he saw light through a tiny crack; and he took his knife and scooped and scooped, until he had made a hole big enough to pass through; then he went out, and came upon a place he had never seen before.

Seeing a path, he followed it until he came to a very large house, the door of which was not fastened. So he went inside, and saw golden doors, with golden locks, and keys of pearl, and beautiful chairs inlaid with jewels and precious stones, and in a reception room he saw a couch covered with a splendid spread, upon which he lay down.

Presently he found himself being lifted off the couch and put in a chair, and heard someone saying: "Do not hurt him; wake him gently," and, on opening his eyes he found himself surrounded by numbers of snakes, one of them wearing beautiful royal colors.

"Hullo!" he cried; "who are you?"

"I am Sultani Wa Nyoka, king of the snakes, and this is my house. Who are you?"

"I am Hassibu Karim Ed Din."

"Where do you come from?"

"I don't know where I come from, or where

I'm going."

"Well, don't bother yourself just now. Let's eat; I guess you are hungry, and I know I am."

Then the king gave orders, and some of the other snakes brought the finest fruits, and they ate and drank and conversed.

When the repast was ended, the king desired to hear Hassibu's story; so he told him all that had happened, and then asked to hear the story of his host.

"Well," said the king of the snakes, "mine is rather a long story, but you shall hear it. A long time ago I left this place, to go and live in the mountains of Al Kaaf, for the change of air. One day I saw a stranger coming along, and I said to him,'Where are you from?' and he said, 'I am wandering in the wilderness.' 'Whose son are you?' I asked. 'My name is Bolukia. My father was a sultan; and when he died I opened a small chest, inside of which I found a bag, which contained a small brass box; when I had opened this I found some writing tied up in a woolen cloth, and it was all in praise of a prophet. He was described as such a good and wonderful

I scared him away

man, that I longed to see him; but when I made inquiries concerning him I was told he was not yet born. Then I vowed I would wander until I should see him. So I left our town, and all my property, and I am wandering, but I have not yet seen that prophet!'

"Then I said to him, 'Where do you expect to find him, if he's not yet born? Perhaps if you had some serpent's water you might keep on living until you find him. But it's of no use talking about that; the serpent's water is too far away.'

"'Well,' he said, 'good-bye. I must wander on.' So I bade him farewell, and he went his way.

"Now, when that man had wandered until he reached Egypt, he met another man, who asked him, 'Who are you?'

"'I am Bolukia. Who are you?'

"'My name is Al Faan. Where are you going?'

"'I have left my home, and my property, and I am seeking the prophet.

"'H'm!' said Al Faan; 'I can tell you of a better occupation than looking for a man that is not born yet. Let us go and find the king of the snakes and get him to give us a charm medicine; then we will go to King Solomon and get his rings, and we shall be able to make slaves of the genii and order them to do whatever we wish.'

"And Bolukia said, 'I have seen the king of the snakes in the mountain of Al Faan'

"'All right,' said Al Faan; 'let's go.'

"Now, Al Faan wanted the ring of Solomon that he might be a great magician and control the genii and the birds, while all Bolukia wanted was to see the great prophet.

"As they went along, Al Faan said to Bolukia, 'Let us make a cage and entice the king of the snakes into it; then we will shut the door and carry him off.'

"'All right,' said Bolukia.

"So they made a cage, and put therein a cup of milk and a cup of wine, and brought it to Al Faan; and I, like a fool, went in, drank up all the wine and became drunk. Then they fastened the door and took me away with them.

"When I came to my senses I found myself in the cage, and Bolukia carrying me, and I said,

'The sons of Adam are no good. What do you want from me?' And they answered, 'We want some medicine to put on our feet, so that we may walk upon the water whenever it is necessary in the course of our journey.' 'Well,' said I, 'go along.'

"We went on until we came to a place where there were a great number and variety of trees; and when those trees saw me, they said, 'I am medicine for this;' 'I am medicine for that; 'I am medicine for the head;' 'I am medicine for the feet;' and presently one tree said, 'If any one puts my medicine upon his feet he can walk on water.'

"When I told that to those men they said, 'That is what we want;' and they took a great deal of it.

"Then they took me back to the mountain and set me free; and we said good-bye and parted.

"When they left me, they went on their way until they reached the sea, when they put the medicine on their feet and walked over. Thus they went many days, until they came near to the place of King Solomon, where they waited while Al Faan prepared his medicines.

"When they arrived at King Solomon's place, he was sleeping, and was being watched by genii, and his hand lay on his chest, with the ring on his finger.

"As Bolukia drew near, one of the genii said to him 'Where are you going?' And he answered, 'I'm here with Al Faan; he's going to take that ring.' 'Go back,' said the genie; 'keep out of the way. That man is going to die.'

"When Al Faan had finished his preparations, he said to Bolukia, 'Wait here for me.' Then he went forward to take the ring, when a great cry arose, and he was thrown by some unseen force a considerable distance.

"Picking himself up, and still believing, in the power of his medicines, he approached the ring again, when a strong breath blew upon him and he was burnt to ashes in a moment.

"While Bolukia was looking at all this, a voice said, 'Go your way; this wretched being is dead.' So he returned; and when he got to the sea again he put the medicine upon his feet and passed over, and continued to wander for many years.

"One morning he saw a man sitting down, and said, 'Good-morning,' to which the man replied. Then Bolukia asked him, 'Who are you?' and he answered: 'My name is Jan Shah. Who are you?' So Bolukia told him who he was, and asked him to tell him his history. The man, who was weeping and smiling by turns, insisted upon hearing Bolukia's story first. After he had heard it he said:

"'Well, sit down, and I'll tell you my story from beginning to end. My name is Jan Shah, and my father is Tuighamus, a great sultan. He used to go every day into the forest to shoot game; so one day I said to him, "Father, let me go with you into the forest to-day;" but he said, "Stay at home. You are better there. "Then I cried bitterly, and as I was his only child, whom he loved dearly, he couldn't stand my tears, so he said: "Very well; you shall go. Don't cry."

"'Thus we went to the forest, and took many attendants with us; and when we reached the place we ate and drank, and then every one set out to hunt.

"'I and my seven slaves went on until we saw a beautiful gazelle, which we chased as far as the sea without capturing it. When the gazelle took to the water I and four of my slaves took a boat, the other three returning to my father, and we chased that gazelle until we lost sight of the shore, but we caught it and killed it. Just then a great wind began to blow, and we lost our way.

"'When the other three slaves came to my father, he asked them, "Where is your master?" and they told him about the gazelle and the boat. Then he cried, "My son is lost! My son is lost!" and returned to the town and mourned for me as one dead.

"'After a time we came to an island, where there were a great many birds. We found fruit and water, we ate and drank, and at night we climbed into a tree and slept till morning.

"'Then we rowed to a second island, and, seeing no one around, we gathered fruit, ate and drank, and climbed a tree as before. During the night we heard many savage beasts howling and roaring near us.

"'In the morning we got away as soon as possible, and came to a third island. Looking around for food, we saw a tree full of fruit like red-streaked apples; but, as we were about to pick some, we heard a voice say, "Don't touch this tree; it belongs to the king." Toward night a number of monkeys came, who seemed much pleased to see us, and they brought us all the fruit we could eat.

"'Presently I heard one of them say, "Let us make this man our sultan." Then another one said: "What's the use? They'll all run away in the morning." But a third one said, "Not if we smash their boat." Sure enough, when we started to leave in the morning, our boat was broken in pieces. So there was nothing for it but to stay there and be entertained by the monkeys, who seemed to like us very much.

"'One day, while strolling about, I came upon a great stone house, having an inscription on the door, which said, "When any man comes to this island, he will find it difficult to leave, because the monkeys desire to have a man for their king. If he looks for a way to escape, he will think there is none; but there is one outlet, which lies to the north. If you go in that direction you will come to a great plain, which is infested with lions, leopards, and snakes. You must fight all of them; and if you overcome them you can go forward. You will then come to another great plain, inhabited by ants as big as dogs; their teeth are like those of dogs and they are very fierce. You must fight these also, and if you overcome them, the rest of the way is clear."

"'1 consulted with my attendants over this information, and we came to the conclusion that, as we could only die, anyhow, we might as well risk death to gain our freedom.

"'As we all had weapons, we set forth; and when we came to the first plain we fought, and two of my slaves were killed. Then we went on to the second plain, fought again; my other two slaves were killed, and I alone escaped.

"'After that I wandered on for many days, living on whatever I could find, until at last I came to a town, where I stayed for some time, looking for employment but finding none.

"One day a man came up to me and said, "Are you looking for work?" "I am," said I. "Come with me, then," said he, and we went to his house.

"'When we got there he produced a camel's skin, and said, "I shall put you in this skin, and a great bird will carry you to the top of yonder mountain. When he gets you there, he will tear this skin off you. You must then drive him away and push down the precious stones you will find there. When they are all down, I wilI get you down."

"'So he put me in the skin; the bird carried me to the top of the mountain and was about to eat me, when I jumped up, scared him away, and then pushed down many precious stones. Then I called out to the man to take me down, but he never answered me, and went away.

"'I gave myself up for a dead man, but went wandering about, until at last, after passing many days in a great forest, I came to a house, all by itself; the old man who lived in it gave me food and drink, and I was revived.

"'I remained there a long time, and that old

man loved me as if I were his own son.

"'One day he went away, and, giving me the keys, told me I could open the door of every room except one which he pointed out to me.

"'Of course, when he was gone, this was the first door I opened. I saw a large garden, through which a stream flowed. Just then three birds came and alighted by the side of the stream. Immediately they changed to three most beautiful women. When they had finished bathing, they put on their clothes, and, as I stood watching them, they changed into birds again and flew away.

"'I locked the door, and went away; but my appetite was gone, and I wandered about aimlessly. When the old man came back, he saw there was something wrong with me, and asked me what was the matter. Then I told him I had seen those beautiful maidens, that I loved one of them very much, and that if I could not marry her I should die.

"'The old man told me I could not possibly have my wish. He said the three lovely beings were the daughters of the sultan of the genii, and that their home was a journey of three years from where we then were.

"'I told him I couldn't help that. He must get her for my wife, or I should die. At last he said, "Well, wait till they come again, then hide yourself and steal the clothes of the one you love so dearly."

"'So I waited, and when they came again I stole the clothes of the youngest, whose name was Sayadati Shems.

"'When they came out of the water, this one could not find her clothes. Then I stepped forward and said, "I have them." "Ah," she begged, "give them to me, their owner; I want to go away." But I said to her, "I love you very much. I want to marry you." I want to go to my father," she replied. "You cannot go," said I.

"'Then her sisters flew away, and I took her into the house, where the old man married us. He told me not to give her those clothes I had taken, but to hide them, because if she ever got them she would fly away to her old home. So I dug a hole in the ground and buried them.

"'But one day, when I was away from home,

she dug them up and put them on; then, saying to the slave I had given her for an attendant, "When your master returns tell him I have gone home; if he really loves me he will follow me," she flew away.

"'When I came home they told me this, and I wandered, searching for her, many years. At last I came to a town where one asked me, "Who are you? "and I answered, "I am Jan Shah." "What was your father's name?" "Tuighamus." "Are you the man who married our mistress?" "Who is your mistress?" "Sayadati Shems." "I am he!" I cried with delight.

"'They took me to their mistress, and she brought me to her father and told him I was her husband; and everybody was happy.

"'Then we thought we should like to visit our old home, and her father's genii carried us there in three days. We stayed there a year and then returned, but in a short time my wife died. Her father tried to comfort me, and wanted me to marry another of his daughters, but I refused to be comforted, and have mourned to this day. That is my story.'

"Then Bolukia went on his way, and wandered till he died."

Next Sultan Wa Nyoka said to Hassibu, "Now, when you go home you will do me injury."

Hassibu was very indignant at the idea, and said, "I could not be induced to do you an injury. Pray, send me home."

"I will send you home," said the king; "but I am sure that you will come back and kill me."

"Why, I dare not be so ungrateful," exclaimed Hassibu. "I swear I could not hurt you."

"Well," said the king of the snakes, "bear this in mind: when you go home, do not go to bathe where there are many people."

And he said, "I will remember." So the king sent him home, and he went to his mother's house, and she was overjoyed to find that he was not dead.

Now, the sultan of the town was very sick; and it was decided that the only thing that could cure him would be to kill the king of the snakes, boil him, and give the soup to the sultan.

For a reason known only to himself, the vizir had placed men at the public baths with this instruction: "If any one who comes to bathe here has a mark on his stomach, seize him and bring him to me."

When Hassibu had been home three days he forgot the warning of Sultani Wa Nyoka, and went to bathe with the other people. All of a sudden he was seized by some soldiers, and brought before the vizier, who said, "Take us to the home of the king of the snakes."

"I don't know where it is," said Hassibu.

"Tie him up," commanded the vizier.

So they tied him up and beat him until his back was all raw, and, being unable to stand the pain he cried, "Let up! I will show you the place."

So he led them to the house of the king of the snakes, who, when he saw him, said, "Didn't I tell you you would come back to kill me?"

"How could I help it?" cried Hassibu. "Look at my back!"

"Who has beaten you so dreadfully?" asked the king.

"The vizier."

"Then there's no hope for me. But you must carry me yourself."

As they went along, the king said to Hassibu, "When we get to your town I shall be killed and cooked. The first skimming the vizier will offer to you, but don't you drink it; put it in a bottle and keep it. The second skimming you must drink, and you will become a great physician. The third skimming is the medicine that will cure your sultan. When the vizier asks you if you drank that first skimming, say, 'I did.' Then produce the bottle containing the first, and say, 'This is the second, and it is for you.' The vizier will take it, and as soon as he drinks it he will die, and both of us will have our revenge."

Everything happened as the king had said. The vizier died, the sultan recovered, and Hassibu was loved by all as a great physician.